Praise for *Worship Not the Creature*

THIS book is so gripping that I found it difficult to put down. I have known Dr. Jones for many years as a physician, hunter, author, and close friend. He and his wife Linda were frequent guests in our home in Washington, D.C., when I was in the U.S. House of Representatives, attending the National Prayer Breakfast and State of the Union Address, among other activities. His beliefs are deep-seated and convincing. Anyone should find this read to be thought-provoking and intensely interesting.

THE HONORABLE J. ROY ROWLAND (D-GA.)
Six-term Congressman, Dublin, Georgia

VERY rarely does a book come out that tackles such an important topic confronting our culture, an issue that is subtle and confounding to many. Dr. Jones does an insightful job of communicating the deception of the animal activist movement that is threatening the very essence of the Judeo-Christian worldview. This is the first book I have read that endeavors to present a true Biblical response to the animal rights agenda. I definitely recommend this book to anyone who wants to better understand this insidious movement and the Biblical viewpoint a Christian should have toward it.

DR. WILLIAM FRANKLIN GRAHAM IV
Billy Graham Evangelistic Association, Charlotte, North Carolina

IN this his newest book, Dr. Jones makes a most compelling and sane case for our proper role in the stewardship of animals. Environmentalists and animal rights activists are well described in Romans 1:25: "For they exchanged the truth of God for a lie, and worshiped and served the creature rather than the Creator." This book is a must-read for anyone who truly cares about God's creation and desires to be equipped to defend truth in the midst of an onslaught of lies.

DALLAS HOLM
Singer, Songwriter, and Outdoorsman, Lindale, Texas

IT seems our politics parallel our theology. Dr. Jones demonstrates how we have allowed the distinction between Creator God and His creation to be blurred or forgotten. I see a very relevant parallel in the way the tenets of American government have also been marginalized as we allow government employees and politicians to contend for unconstitutional disarmament of American citizens. Jones rightly sees this attempt to transfer sovereignty from the people to the government as apocalyptic.

LARRY PRATT
Executive Director, Gun Owners of America, Springfield, Virginia

DR. JONES is one of our most popular authors in *Sports Afield* and at Safari Press books. *Worship Not the Creature: Animal Rights and the Bible* is a book that should make all reasonable people seriously think. If you believe animal rights activists are joking when they say that riding a horse is a violation of its rights, you had better read this book. The radical fringe of the animal rights movement is deadly serious about passing its agenda. We had better wake up quickly!

LUDO WURFBAIN
Publisher, Safari Press and *Sports Afield,* Huntington Beach, California

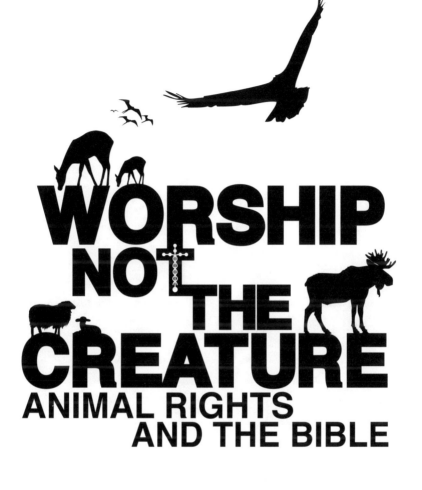

WORSHIP NOT THE CREATURE

ANIMAL RIGHTS
AND THE BIBLE

J.Y. Jones

Nordskog
Publishing inc.

VENTURA, CALIFORNIA

Worship Not the Creature:
Animal Rights and the Bible

by J. Y. Jones, M.D.

International Standard Book Number: 978-0-9824929-1-8
Library of Congress Control Number: 2009930617

Theology Editor: Ronald W. Kirk
Manuscript Editor: Kimberley Winters Woods
Typography, Design, and Editing: Desta Garrett
Cover Design: Aaron Ford, Digicom Designs
Cover Photographs by J. Y. Jones
Author Photograph by Linda Jones

Printed in the United States of America,

Published by

Nordskog Publishing, Inc.
2716 Sailor Avenue
Ventura, California 93001, USA
1-805-642-2070 • 1-805-276-5129
www.NordskogPublishing.com

Member

Christian Small Publishers Association

CONTENTS

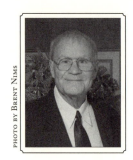

PUBLISHER'S WORD

Gerald Christian Nordskog

M<small>Y</small> Sicilian grandfather's sister was a vegetarian living on her avocado ranch in Oceanside, California, in the middle of the twentieth century. At that time, she was the only one I knew. Today, there are more vegans than ever before. Many promote it as a healthier diet and lifestyle, but some vegetarians may be promoting a deeper, hidden agenda. In this book, Dr. Jones exposes vegetarianism—especially political activists—with facts and truth. He also brings to light the radical agendas driving the environmentalist and animal rights movements, especially in contrast to the Christian premise of responsible stewardship of animals as revealed in Scripture, building his case upon the God-approved and God-sanctioned uses of animals as beasts of burden and as food. His analysis of the false Darwinian theory of evolution versus God's creation as recorded in Genesis is brilliant. And the difference between macro and micro evolutionary models is very important to understand. Further, as an ophthalmologist and surgeon, his description of the intricacies and brilliance of God's design and creation of the eye and eyesight found in Chapter One (pp. 9-10) is priceless!

This book is vital today to expose the unbiblical agenda of the so-called animal rights movement, which often acts in concert with radical environmentalism. This is a serious book which lays bare the insane arguments propagated in the media on a near-daily basis. Read what the Bible, God's Word, says about the intended and proper care, use, and treatment of animals. This is long overdue in today's man-centered and animal-centered culture. Are we to worship the creature more than the Creator of the universe? Are we to hold up the animal kingdom as more important than "the image-bearer" and our Creator in Heaven? What does Holy Scripture say about these things?

A word of caution: The doomsday predictions and apocalyptic opinions of the author, while very popular today through books and movies, is not our understanding of Bible prophecy and its partial fulfillment that we believe has already occurred. We disagree with much of the end-times scenarios of this book, especially chapters 12 and 13, which represent the author's opinion based upon his interpretation of theology and eschatology. It is not our view, as you will also see in the Theology Editor's Word by Ronald W. Kirk, which follows this Foreword. We are not inclined to believe that wild beasts will run rampant and devour humans wholesale—although Leviticus 26:22 was the Lord's warning to the Israelites to be obedient to His commandments or face the consequences of the curse, and Revelation 6:8 does warn unbelievers [particularly] of these consequences being unleashed.

Personally, I believe the Beast was first-century Roman-emperor Nero who greatly persecuted the Christians (among other tyrannical dastardly deeds) leading up to the destruction of Jerusalem and the old (Jewish) sacrificial system in A.D. 70. However, we advise readers to seek the truth by intensive study of the Word of God. I also recommend to you another, more optimistic, book published by NPI for further study: Dr. Greg Uttinger's *A Whole New World: The Gospel According to Revelation*.

As Romans 1:24-25 warns, do not be trapped into the lie of worshipping and serving the creature while forsaking the Creator. Worship our Triune Lord God and serve Him all the days of your life.

Jesus proclaims the truth,

"I am alpha and Omega,
the beginning and the end, the first and the last.
Blessed are they, that do His Commandments,
that their right may be in the tree of Life,
and may enter in through the gates into the City."
(Revelation 22:13-14, Geneva Bible, 1599).

Theology
Editor's Word
Ronald W. Kirk

Worship Not the Creature: Animal Rights and the Bible is the striking product of an amazing man. J. Y. Jones is an old-fashioned fellow—a Christian, a scholar and a man of action. He is both humble as the day is long, and as forthright—and apparently tough—as anyone. He is a man's man. Accordingly, in this work on the Biblical treatment of animals as against the views of the radical animal rights movement, he bravely treats a politically volatile subject.

Here is Dr. Jones's proposition: Working in conjunction with its close allies in the radical environmental movement, the animal rights movement seems to be gaining momentum, power, and influence all over the United States and Western Europe. This movement has migrated completely away from issues of animal stewardship and now calls for a wholesale halt to all animal utilization to meet any human needs. This trend is linked to a dangerous form of radical vegetarianism, the logical outcome of such a philosophy. The movement touts all aspects of its plan for humanity as good for people, the environment, and for animals. In recent years, increasing numbers of articles, websites, and books have attempted to give credence to their radical philosophies, supposedly using the Holy Bible to support their arguments.

All such attempts to make these radical philosophies appear "God-sanctioned" are highly in error and beg a scholarly attempt to refute them. This is essentially what *Worship Not the Creature: Animal Rights and the Bible* is all about.

The apocalyptic nature of *Worship Not the Creature* requires a bit of an explanation. Eschatology—the study of end-times—is necessarily a speculative endeavor because we seek to understand things yet to happen on the basis of Biblical revelation written in perhaps obscure terms. We see through a glass darkly, as the Apostle Paul said in 1 Corinthians 13:12. In contrast to the more popular premillennial eschatology of Dr. Jones, based upon our reasoned conviction, Nordskog Publishing, Inc. (NPI), presumes a postmillennial view. In the postmillennial model, the Last Days (to use the Biblical term) began with the resurrection of Christ. According to Psalm 110, Christ then reigned and now reigns at the right hand of the Father, in the midst of His foes, where He will stay until His enemies are vanquished. And the last enemy is death (1 Corinthians 15:26). Christ executes His rule through his volunteers—Christians. In the postmillennial view, through the power of the Holy Spirit mankind is increasingly evangelized unto salvation, producing ever greater fruit. In the postmillennial view, upon the success of the Holy Spirit's ministry to convert men, the internal kingdom of Christ expresses itself in greater and greater spheres until the whole earth is filled with His glory (e.g., Psalm 72:19; Isaiah 54:5-8); for of the increase of His government, there is no end (Isaiah 9:7). The postmillennialist argues that if Christ must return in person to establish His kingdom with a rod of iron against an overwhelmingly rebellious earth, then His kingdom is an external kingdom, much like all Israel believed and sought of Him, including Jesus' disciples at His first coming. Again, the postmillennialist does indeed believe, as the Scripture says, that He rules with a rod of iron, but, again, through His people, through the increasing power of Christian influence. In spite of apparent historical set-backs, as in the present age, the postmillennial believer trusts God's plan. The kingdom comes without observation (Luke 17:20-21).

Such was the conviction of the early American Pilgrim and Puritan. This conviction produced the great outworking of faith that led to the creation of the United States, as early Americans self-consciously sought to be instruments of Christ in the world—a city set on a hill. As the

nation increasingly abandoned historic postmillennialism, with its doctrines of civil responsibility and stewardship, the United States has come
to be increasingly ruled by godless and ambitious men. As Scripture
warns, "When the wicked rule, the people groan" (Proverbs 29:2). Thus,
one might argue that our current decline and potential for apocalyptic
judgment may be, at least in part, the direct result of a faulty eschatology.

Why in the world would Nordskog Publishing undertake a book
grounded so thoroughly upon what is to us a faulty eschatology? The
answer is simple and profound: Whether or not the premillennial view
of Dr. Jones or the postmillennial view is correct, it appears clear that the
more successful the radical animal rights movement becomes, the more
apocalyptic proportions of evil will be the result—at least in the short
run. In other words, every Christian eschatology properly embraces the
law of consequences. Upon our conversations with him, we believe that
Dr. Jones agrees: Irresponsibility on the part of Christians is a very bad
way to bring in the end times. We would not be like the foolish virgins
of Matthew 25. Therefore, at root, we seek the same result. Christians
must be aware of the schemes of those who would undermine our faith,
and be prepared to answer God's call to action, by faith, and finally let
Him bring the increase as He wills.

Therefore, while we may disagree with certain specific assertions in
Worship Not the Creature, NPI overwhelmingly endorses the primary
theme: The animal rights movement is dangerous, contradicts the fundamental Biblical notion that men are more valuable than many sparrows,
and holds the potential for devastating evil among men.

With a whole heart we recommend *Worship Not the Creature* to all
serious Christians and seekers as food for thought, and perhaps the very
remedy in Christian understanding and action that will reverse the trend
toward barbaric paganism that the animal rights movement represents.

INTRODUCTION

For more than sixteen years I've been working and reworking what I hope will be a masterpiece fiction novel that exposes the animal rights movement for what it is: A colossal corruption of the God-given mandate that man exercise authority over the creation, including the utilization of animals. I have woven into that book a possible scenario that culminates with the victorious animal rights movement in control of the world, displaying full force all its fury and intolerance. This futuristic novel, titled *Lightspeed to Babylon*, is intense and requires more than the usual degree of concentration by the reader. The book now in your hands contains many of the scriptural principles I used to formulate *Lightspeed to Babylon*, but in a nonfiction format that is relatively uncomplicated.

The Christian community in general, unfortunately, seems to have little appreciation for the significance of the animal rights movement. There appears to be very little perceived threat and virtually no solid Biblical teaching on the subject. A search of the internet reveals a smattering of accurate and useful sites and articles, but the number is dwarfed by the tide of animal rights and vegetarian propaganda, not to mention tons of radical environmentalist sites, a sizable portion of which wrongly utilize the Bible in an attempt to substantiate their claims.

The animal rights movement seems to be gaining momentum, power, and influence all over the United States and Western Europe, working in conjunction with its close allies in the radical environmental movement. It has moved completely away from issues of animal stewardship and now calls for a wholesale halt to all animal utilization to meet any human needs. This trend is linked to a dangerous form of radical vegetarianism, the logical outcome of such a philosophy. The movement touts all aspects of its plan for humanity as good for people, the environment, and animals. While the Bible unquestionably teaches good stewardship of animals under man's dominion, it is highly deceptive and absolutely erroneous to use it in support of arguments for animal rights.

All such attempts to make these radical philosophies "God-sanctioned" are highly in error and beg a scholarly attempt to refute them. That is essentially what this book is all about.

The first chapter shows how godless evolution is scientifically indefensible as the origin of the cosmos, and that it is impotent in its ability to create life or new species. It also demonstrates, by personal example, how its teaching leads to degradation of the lives of individuals and of society at large. This initial part of the book also strongly defends the integrity and veracity of the Bible. All these elements are necessary to mount an effective opposition to today's animal rights movement.

Subsequent chapters trace the human/animal relationship from the time of creation all the way to the time of the predicted apocalypse. This material strongly defends traditional animal stewardship as God-ordained and God-sanctioned from creation to the time when Christ reigns supreme on earth. I draw out a host of little-understood concepts to show that both the radical animal rights and environmental movements are apocalyptic aberrations counter to God's will, and are well-predicted in the Holy Bible.

Christians may feel down deep that something isn't exactly right when it comes to the concept of animal rights, but too frequently they don't know how to express it, much less how to counter it effectively. It isn't just those in the pews who are confused, either. I personally know a number of Christian leaders who shy away from the topic, even keeping a low profile when it comes to their passionate love for hunting and the outdoors. In certain circumstances, they might even hide their love for a ham sandwich for fear of criticism (and maybe a loss of support) from opponents. I find this to be a subtle form of hypocrisy that ignores Biblical truth (such as Romans 12:1-2) and instead conforms to what is becoming increasingly viewed by society at large as "correct thinking."

I do have premillennial leanings. In interpreting the Scriptures, I have diligently attempted not to take an extreme and uncompromising view regarding any of the mainstream eschatological (future things) positions prevalent in the Christian community, of which there are at least four. In some places there are allusions to one variation or another, so the Christian reader who feels strongly in favor of a differing view is urged to *let love cover a multitude of transgressions* (Proverbs 10:12; 1 Peter 4:8). Please remember that this is not a book on eschatology, and I am pushing no particular interpretation as the "correct" one. However, the premillennial view fits some of my conclusions best in some places, though there is obviously room for honest, brotherly disagreement.

Many of the scenarios constructed in my novel, *Lightspeed to Babylon*, have already come to pass, even though the novel is set approximately one hundred years in the future. Recently, a television program showed starving children scraping up stray grains of rice from the floor of a threshing house in Thailand, coming very close to fulfilling a scene in my novel. News of the latest wild-animal attack, another prediction in *Lightspeed to Babylon*, has become so frequent I can't even begin to catalog it. Also, there have been constant disputes between seven states of the USA that share water rights to the Colorado River in deep conflict over that vital resource, a disagreement that erupts into open war in my novel. Another quarrel has raged over Chattahoochee River water rights, featuring my home state of Georgia in disagreement with Alabama and Florida. Often I sit and watch television news programs in astonishment as another outlandish prediction comes to life before my eyes. This shouldn't surprise me, since the whole book is based on my viewpoint of prophecies in God's Word, but still I'm awed. Consequently, I am grateful to NPI for their willingness to publish this book.

While the connection may not be obvious to the casual observer, it is my firm conviction that the Christian community, as well as the world at large, is being blindsided by the animal rights movement, in concert with its allies in the radical environmental movement. The Biblical predictions about these movements are so vivid and real that one should not be surprised they are linked. These two camps are birds of a feather, and I intend to make this clear in the pages to follow.

Please remember that I am not a chemist, biologist, geologist, or astronomer; however, I have studied all these disciplines to some extent and have a working knowledge that I believe is sufficient for this work. I am a practicing physician with a good background in basic sciences, and I am capable of understanding the fundamentals of all of these. I have researched my statements both in the pertinent literature and on hundreds of internet sites, surveying both the pros and the cons when it comes to my premises, to the extent that I am comfortable with my allegations. Where there is any doubt or sincere, science-based disagreement, I have tried to indicate this so the reader isn't led into drawing shaky conclusions. I make this statement because this book is certain to come under scrutiny from the anti-God faction, whose internet sites are rife with harsh criticism of any literalist interpretation of the Bible.

As for animal rights activism and radical environmentalism, please make no mistake, Christians. This is war, and if you stay asleep we will quickly lose. The return of Christ will solve all such problems but, in the meantime, we must live our lives with our eyes open and do the work of building His Kingdom. I believe that the animal rights movement* is the enemy of all Christ stands for, and a manifestation of the true spirit of the Antichrist.

EDITOR'S NOTES:

All Biblical quotations in this work are taken from the New American Standard Bible (NASB). One should note that many times the word "meat" is used in the King James Version where in contemporary vernacular it would now be translated "food" or "meal." Appropriately for today's handling of the term, modern translations generally render it according to modern usage as "food" in the modern sense. Where the actual word for meat is used in the Greek, in most modern translations it is translated as "meat."

* The compound-modifer hyphen in the phrase "animal-rights…" is intentionally left out by the author to reflect usage in contemporary public discourse.

ONE

CREATION, EVOLUTION, AND BIBLICAL INTEGRITY

Personal Background

I WAS born poor in the remote mountains of northern Georgia. My father was a career soldier who was very often away from home, and I lived some years with my mother and her parents in a house without electricity, indoor plumbing, or running water. My grandfather Anderson, my mother's father, was a farmer who spent many long days walking behind a horse-drawn plow. I witnessed animal stewardship and animal utilization up close from the time I could walk. I took a trip to town with "Pa" Anderson every Saturday on a one-horse wagon, our only means of transportation at the time. I witnessed "hog-killing time" from the .22 bullet between the pig's eyes to the final rendering of chunks of fat into lard. I watched my mother and grandmother prepare Sunday dinner many times, with the first step being to wring the neck of one of the farmyard chickens. I sometimes went with my grandfather to the woods in back of the farmhouse where we shot a squirrel or two and then I "helped" as he skinned them for the pot. There was no sterile packaging in those days to blur and confuse one about the origin of meat. In our situation one could easily witness the whole process from living creature to hot meat on the plate, a common experience in what was at the time principally an agrarian society.

I am certain this is one reason many people today are so exceptionally susceptible to the concept of animal rights. They can have a hamburger at McDonald's and never consider that an animal died to create that bun-wrapped piece of meat. They can wear leather shoes, belts and watchbands, and never have it occur to them that these are animal products. I have heard this same argument made far more eloquently than I am capable of doing, so I won't go into it in more detail. But remember that our disconnection from the land is truly playing into the hands of those who would deceive us with the concept of animal rights. By the above observation, I am not suggesting that the *leaders* of the animal rights movement are necessarily hypocrites in this matter because they are true fanatics, and fanatics will go to extremes in an attempt to demonstrate their point and their sincerity. I would, however, submit that a large majority of their followers and contributors are unaware of the drastic implications of the movement as a whole. What many of these deceived people fail to realize is that one cannot have rights unless there is counterbalancing responsibility. This is true in every area of life, and the irresponsible person often loses rights by committing some crime that sends him or her to prison. While some species of animals can be trained to perform reliably many valuable tasks, they are incapable of exercising responsibility so, by definition, they cannot have human-like rights.

I became a Christian at age 16 at a revival at a local Baptist church. As seems all too common in many denominations, I was expected afterward to be fully grown in my faith and have all the answers I needed. I never heard a true teaching sermon until almost twenty years later but, as a youth, I regularly heard the Gospel and was once more evangelized every time I went to church. Today evangelism is one of my own passions, but back then I had already heard it told many times and in many different ways, yet I still struggled with the same impulses I had endured before I had gone down to the altar. When I went off to college at age 17, I was basically untaught in any Biblical doctrine except for the fundamentals of the Gospel. I knew very little about the many guidelines for living a happy and fulfilling life that have since come alive for me on the pages of the Bible. It is an odd thing, but many, if not most, of these guidelines run counter to our natural inclinations. That is probably why Jesus' teaching was so radical. I've stated before and I believe it's true: Doing what comes naturally is usually the wrong thing to do. The natural man (or woman) hasn't the capacity to make godly choices until Christ takes up residence in their heart by His Spirit (1 Corinthians 2:14–16).

A Fall from Faith

At this juncture, my young faith began to be replaced by doubt, a malady that was reinforced by both my college peers and, more effectively, by many of my college professors. I firmly believe, after recovering from a near-fatal downward spiral that lasted fifteen years, that every person on planet Earth, as well as every person who has ever lived, is a builder. They are either building faith or else they are building doubt. For all my college, medical school, and army years, as well as most of my specialty training time, I was building doubt.

It was in my second year of college that I started my numerous biology courses under a brilliant professor who also became a fishing friend and a mentor in the nuances of evolution. In our informal times together I questioned him about matters of faith and he maintained (and I know he believed it) that there was no conflict between evolution and the concept of God. This assertion has only recently been given official acceptance by many mainstream Christian churches, with television host John Ankerberg leading the movement by citing "new scientific information" that is really nothing more than the ancient day/age theory originally put forth in 1814 by Scottish theologian Thomas Chalmers.[1, 2] In Chalmers' treatise, as with all subsequent refinements of this erroneous doctrine, a futile attempt is made to harmonize the book of Genesis with conventional deep-time and ancient-earth theories. Such efforts at compromise never convince committed evolutionists to believe the Bible is true. Moreover, this kind of "bargain with the Devil" injects into sincere Christians a measure of doubt, because such an untenable position does nothing more than undermine Biblical integrity.

My professor's assurances made me feel only a little better, and the college education I received greatly reinforced my own skepticism about what had occurred when I became a Christian. Worse, what little I knew about the Bible appeared to be at great odds with the fundamentals of evolution. Being quite pragmatic, and quite trusting of learned people, I easily deduced that such matters as instantaneous creation by God, men living to be hundreds of years old, a worldwide flood, and numerous other tales found in the Bible could be no more than fanciful imaginations penned by some near-mad writer many centuries ago. I decided that there must be a God and that through a mysterious mechanism I didn't understand there must be hope of eternal life in Jesus' name. At the same time, I also decided the Bible had to contain numerous errors and thus could not be completely trusted. It took only a little figuring to decide that any inconvenient conflict between the Bible and my newly entrenched evolutionary worldview could be dismissed.

I married my wife, Linda, while we were both sophomores in college. In those early years, we went to separate schools and saw one another only for an occasional weekend. I even went to medical school a year early, after only three years of college, and lived in a fraternity house while Linda completed her education to become an English teacher. After that, we lived together in a tiny house and had our first child before I finished medical school. Although a faithful husband, the thought gnawed at me that there really was no real basis for this one-man/one-woman relationship. For a rising young doctor with a head full of curly hair, beautiful girls were easily available if one happened to be so inclined. I had heard that marriage was to be a lifelong thing, but to me it appeared increasingly disposable. After all, if the Bible was wrong on such basic concepts as creation, evolution, the purported worldwide flood, and men living to impossible ages, it could very well be wrong on less cosmic points. My doubts caused my marriage to teeter chronically on the edge of disaster but, by God's grace alone, it held together.

I did my year of service in Vietnam as soon as my internship was over, fulfilling the duties of an army flight surgeon. While in Vietnam, I was quite popular with the local Vietnamese population as a "bac-see," or doctor, since I was always available to see them and treat their many ailments. I faced myriad temptations during that tour and, partially to counterbalance the problem, I corresponded extensively with Linda, never faltering in my love for her, and I even called her every time opportunity presented. Through it all, my meditations were anything but holy, and I knew that I was caught in somewhat of a double life. Still, I had few thoughts that anything I did (and perhaps anything anybody else did, for that matter) was wicked or abhorrent. Base impulses in me and the men under my charge were natural, and my belief in evolution and the many supposed errors in the Bible allowed for few pangs of conscience. After all, believing I had descended from animals, even if the line had been guided by the hand of God, gave me no reason for modification of thought or behavior based on any error-tainted ancient book.

On my return from Vietnam, I was accepted into the U.S. Army ophthalmology residency at Walter Reed Army Medical Center in Washington, D.C. I resumed my life with Linda, and somehow most of my more ignoble inclinations became a thing of the past. Temptations were still there, of course, as they are today, abating little even for a man who is now of Medicare age. My basic philosophy and worldview hadn't changed that first year at Walter Reed, but something told me I needed to turn over a new leaf (a strategy I now know is always doomed to failure), and become more responsible for the good of my family and children. However humanistic my strategy, I believe this constituted the beginning of a true change of heart in me, perhaps a long-suppressed work of the Holy Spirit. We now had our second child, born while we were at Walter Reed. I believe I was a good ophthalmology resident and I had a talent for surgery that was apparent from the start. Still, true satisfaction eluded me, though I couldn't yet put my finger on the reasons why.

A Miraculous Recovery—Saved by Science

At the end of my first year of training, my class of residents was sent to Colby College in Waterville, Maine, for basic science classes in all aspects of visual function. The course lasted all summer and it was a wonderful time, with many recreational opportunities and no duties requiring night call or seeing patients. Instead, we went to school every day with other ophthalmology residents from around the world to learn the basics of what makes the eye tick, including biochemistry, optics, and the like. I absorbed the material with greatest interest, but one particular section really caught my attention.

I remember listening to the professor explain how light enters the eye, passes through several types of clear material, and then strikes the back of the eye to produce a chemical change in the photoreceptors, the elements that actually pick up the stimulus. This complicated chemical reaction triggers a neural impulse, and this is fired along the retinal nerve-fiber layer, which is gathered into the optic nerve of each eye. This structure passes out the back of the eye and then through a hole in the bone at the apex of the orbit. After that, it crosses the other optic nerve at the optic chiasm beneath the brain, where the fibers are divided into those coming from the right side of both eyes and those coming from the left side of both eyes. In the normal individual, this crossover allows a person to see all things to the left and all things to the right at once. The tracts, or nerve pathways, formed by this division go to the temporal region on each side of the brain to enter a structure known as the lateral geniculate body where they synapse (hand off the impulse to a different nerve cell), and then these pass to the very back of the brain to the occipital lobe, the area responsible for processing incoming visual information. Finally, the occipital lobe notifies the cerebral cortex of the visual information, allowing what started out as a beam of light to be perceived consciously as vision.

The above is a severely abbreviated description of what we learned, which was plenty enough to get me into thinking mode. Almost in an instant, I became convicted that there is a very real God out there who intentionally made this incredible body in which we are housed for the few brief years of our life. I had studied complicated body processes before, of course, while in medical school. Somehow, though, God chose this spectacular aspect of creation to reveal Himself to me personally in a way I had never before known. I walked out of one of the classes with a completely different mindset, and with a determination to seek out and learn more about this God who could create such a work of genius. I knew a little about the Bible from long-ago sermons, though I had never read it, yet something told me that it was the right place to start.

My search has led me on many journeys and has revealed to me infinitely more real, lasting knowledge than all my previous course work. I began shortly thereafter to read the Bible on my own and, some years later, I came under the tutelage of a mature Christian brother. I became interested in the works of the Institute for Creation Research (www.icr.

org), and I discovered that not only did evolution not occur, it *could not occur* under any conceivable set of circumstances. Thus, my belief in a Creator God became deeper and stronger. I had begun building faith instead of doubt for the first time since I went off to college as a teenager.

Evolution *Can't* Be!

As one secular authority puts it, "It should be clear that the claim for an inherent evolutionary increase in entropy and organization [I believe this source meant to state *decrease in entropy and increase in organization—* brackets mine] is based on an arbitrary model which shows signs of having been constructed simply to yield the desired result.... There is nothing in evolutionary or developmental biology that justifies their assumptions that a successful mutation...is always associated with an increase in some global measure of phenotype. Nor is there anything to support the assumption that new species arise as the result of single gene mutations.... If these assumptions are removed, the whole edifice collapses."[3]

This is a complicated way of saying that the theory of evolution has been constructed on a very shaky framework, and that its proponents know it. I believe this is the main source of the intense resistance that exists to a side-by-side comparison between evolution and creation in the classroom. Creationism is disparaged as unscientific, backwards, and ignorant, and the very idea is subjected to all manner of scornful attacks. What its opponents refuse to recognize is that *if* indeed God created, then the theory of evolution represents the epitome of ignorant drivel. When scrutinized alongside the more viable alternative with all the facts and statistics laid bare, I believe almost anyone with an open mind will reject evolution and embrace creation. That is why teaching creationism in the public arena as a scientific alternative is so vehemently opposed by evolutionists. Their pet theory simply can't take the heat!

An example of this is found in an incisive work I'd recommend to all who crave the truth about the matter of evolution.[4] In that book, a molecular biologist studying DNA is quoted, and he states regarding its origin, "Nobody in my profession truly believes it evolved. It was engineered by 'genius beyond genius,' and such information could not have been written in any other way. The paper and ink did not write the book.... To be a molecular biologist *requires one to hold two insanities at all times* [italics mine]. One, it would be insane to believe in evolution when you can see the truth for yourself. Two, it would be insane to say you don't believe in evolution. All government work, research grants, papers, big college lectures—everything would stop. I'd be out of a job.... Design, it's like the elephant in the living room. It moves around, takes up an enormous amount of space, loudly trumpets, bumps into us, knocks things over, eats a ton of hay, and smells like an elephant. And yet we have to swear it isn't there."[5]

Entropy is the opposite of organization. It constitutes the condition where energy is no longer available to do work. Because the universe would "wind down" without constant replenishment, it should be materially demonstrable that the universe requires God's input of energy to maintain it. The creation itself literally cries out that there is a Creator. I have never seen or heard a scientifically proven fact that contradicts this truth.

The reason evolution is impossible is based on a number of major factors, among which is the paucity of time, even under the most optimistic evolutionary scenarios. Quoting again the scientific literature, "The question of how fast the U.S. land mass is being washed into the sea has been given a new answer by two Princeton University geologists, Sheldon Judson and Dale F. Ritter. They calculate that solid and dissolved material carried by the rivers of the USA is sufficient to lower the average land surface by 2.4 inches in 1,000 years, a rate about twice as high as previous estimates.... Taking the average height of the United States above sea level as 2,300 feet and assuming that the rates of erosion reported here are representative, we find that it would take 11 to 12 million years to move to the oceans a volume equivalent to that of the United States lying above sea level. At this rate there has been enough time since the Cretaceous [which supposedly ended sixty-five million years ago—brackets mine] to destroy such a land mass six times over."[6]

The second law of thermodynamics is often cited as evidence that evolution cannot have occurred. One authority puts it this way: "The whole notion that random change over a long period of time can transform simple systems into ever more complex systems runs precisely contrary to one of the most fundamental laws of nature—the Second Law of Thermodynamics. The Second Law states that with time, everything in the universe tends to undergo progressive degradation. With the passing of time, things do not naturally increase in order and complexity—they decrease. Think of what spontaneous change over a thousand years will do to an automobile, or your own body. Scientists tell us that with enough time, this natural degradation process will lead to the 'heat death' of the whole universe when virtually everything in nature will run down to the point that even molecular motion will cease."[7] Apart from God's supernatural input of energy, this eventuality might well have already come to pass.

While a temporary reversal of entropy does occur in living systems to allow seeds to germinate, animals to reproduce and grow, and the like, these all require an incredibly complex system that *already includes* a directed energy source, a template for replication, and a replication mechanism. This could only occur if constructed intentionally by "genius beyond genius," as the molecular biologist quoted above notes. Chemicals that form components of living systems must also have protection from powerful external degradation forces, usually supplied by the intricate cell membrane. Only in living cells are all these components found. The postulated reversal of this fundamental law to allow spontaneous development of life, and then for increasing complexity of organisms, is thus impossible, supplying positive proof that Darwinian and neo-Darwinian evolution cannot have occurred.

Another objection to evolution is the mathematics of chance, which weigh in overwhelmingly (to put it very mildly) against the accidental occurrence of life. Most scientists who still believe in evolution (unfortunately an exceedingly hard-headed majority) apparently never consider this huge roadblock, or else they explain it away, often by such convoluted reasoning that it can only be seen through the eyes of faith—misplaced faith in something that *can't* be. Michael Behe's best-selling 1996 book, *Darwin's Black Box* (The Free Press, a division of Simon & Schuster, Inc., New York), contains some of the best illustrations of how unworkable is the concept of evolution. Behe touts the "irreducible complexity" of living structures, citing examples mainly from the human body, where critical processes such as cellular function and blood clotting cannot occur without all the necessary steps, microscopic organelles, chemicals, and enzymes already in place. Since there is no way to arrive at these functions in stepwise fashion, as required by evolution, it is obvious that it cannot have happened by accident.

It isn't just in the human body that this barrier to evolution is found, either. In all of creation one finds innumerable examples, such that irreducible complexity is the rule and exceptions to it are rare, if they exist at all. Behe is quite secular in his beliefs, and his apparent conclusion is erroneous, since he seems to believe that cells are so complicated they had to be seeded on Earth by some advanced, higher intelligence (or accidentally by comets) to evolve into today's complex array of living systems found here. The technical name for this unlikely scenario is "directed panspermia," an idea popularized by the knighted British astronomer Fred Hoyle. The question as to where *those* advanced creatures originated is left begging by both Behe and Hoyle. However, Behe has certainly dissected and catalogued well why evolution as a product of chance cannot have occurred in any imaginable manner, and that seeking alternative explanations is indicated. Hoyle, in fact, was so convinced that life could not have arisen spontaneously by classical Darwinian mechanisms that he made the statement, "The Darwinian theory is wrong and the continued adherence to it is an impediment to discovering the correct evolutionary theory."[8]

Mathematicians and evolutionists have been at odds for decades over whether life (and indeed all matter) could have evolved spontaneously due to random changes, and Hoyle, who is now deceased, found himself in the thick of the controversy. The whole question mainly originated in the 1960s, with the advent of computers and improved ability to do higher mathematics faster and more accurately. Beyond question, the mathematical fact is that evolution could not have occurred spontaneously.[9] One scientist has stated, "Molecular biology may well have provided us with the alphabet of this language, but it is a long step from the alphabet to understanding a language.... A language has to have rules, and these are the strongest constraints on the set of possible messages. No currently existing formal language can tolerate random changes in the symbol sequences which express its sentences. Meaning is almost invariably destroyed. Any changes must be syntactically lawful ones. I would conjecture that what one might call 'genetic grammaticality' has a deterministic explanation and does not owe its stability to selection pressure acting on random variation." [10]

Again, this is a scientific way of saying that evolution by chance cannot have occurred, and that alternative explanations should be sought.

One need not cling to the biological sciences to refute evolution. The Solar system and the entire universe are overflowing with phenomena that could not have occurred by chance. Even the distribution of matter in the cosmos is far from random, so in like manner inanimate nonliving heavenly bodies fit this rule of irreducible complexity. The "lumpiness" of the universe has always been problematic for "big bang" theories, which are now shifting to concepts that defy proving, like cosmic "dark matter." As one scientist says, "We are perplexed at the order that is such an elementary part of the universe in which we live. There should instead be disarray, it seems much more logical, for we naturally consider the infinity of chaotic universes that could exist in place of the one ordered and systematic universe that is present." [11]

Translation: An uncontrolled explosion like the "big bang" could never create our complex and ordered universe. Even the gorgeous array of dissimilar bodies we find in our own solar system defies explanation. No two major planets or moons are the same, and it is the dissimilarities that are absolutely striking. Few people understand how difficult it is to achieve a perfectly elliptical orbit for a manmade satellite. Despite this, numerous planetary and lunar orbits in the Solar system approach being perfectly elliptical, a condition which is infinitely unlikely to have occurred by chance from collisions between heavenly bodies. Even more complicated are such phenomena as widely-dispersed and infinitely varied galaxies and interstellar gases, as well as clusters and systems of galaxies.

The young age of the universe (and more specifically our earth-moon system) can be proved to be no more than 1.2 billion years old by the recession rate of the moon. The moon is receding from the earth at a rate of 3.82 centimeters per year. Extrapolating backward at a constant rate, and assuming the moon started out at only 15,000 miles above the surface of the earth, one gets an age of only 1.2 billion years. However, such a near position for the moon is impossible, since gravitational tides on earth would be eight miles high at that point, and both the planet and the moon would be stressed to the point of possible rupture by gravity. Thus, the earth-moon system must be much younger than 1.2 billion years. A more complete discussion of this irrefutable fact is found in Dr. Walt Brown's book.

On the basis of the scientific evidence alone, I rapidly settled into the belief system of a creationist, my joyous new worldview which I scrutinized intently and skeptically at first, only to discover it was the only plausible explanation for the complexity and diversity of nature. I initially based my new strict creationist worldview not on the Bible, but instead on the more familiar dictates of science. It was amazing for me to discover that my new thinking was perfectly aligned with the Bible. The only exception to this is what I'll accurately call speculative science, that is, the study of non-provable concepts that intentionally leave a Creator God out of the equation. Evolution is at the top of the list of such unscientific nonsense, a fact I simply couldn't see before my own epiphany at Colby College. The change in mindset drastically altered every phase of my life, and solidified my marriage as perhaps nothing else could have. I couldn't realize it while it was happening, but my whole problem was caused by mistrust of the Bible and its contents.

What godless modernists call "science" is historically called natural philosophy, which is actually no more than a belief system. It is based upon pre-existing premises of thought, better known as presuppositions. Everyone possesses the unavoidable bias of presupposition, which the classic scientific method diligently seeks to eliminate (double-blind studies such as are used in medicine to prevent intrusion of bias in evaluating drug effects, where neither the patient nor the doctor knows if the patient is taking actual medication or a placebo, for example). When presuppositions are *intentionally* applied so as to circumvent the tested and true scientific method of falsifiability, or the ability to duplicate an experiment and obtain repeatable results in order to prove whether it is true or not, then the supposed objectivity of modern science is totally destroyed. What the "science" of evolution has become is an unmitigated lie, and to the thinking person it is offensive as well as intellectually disingenuous and even intolerable.

While practically all highbrow orthodox evolutionists scoff at creationism, it is actually they who are so entrenched in evolutionary philosophy that they never stop to think whether they might be entirely wrong, and if in fact evolutionary theory under unbiased scrutiny has any chance of being true. How many former creationists do you know who now embrace evolution? Perhaps one or two, but they are rare. On the other hand, former evolutionists like me who hold a doctorate, and who have taken the time to explore the rich, fertile field of creationism and have there found the truth, are a dime a dozen. This growing number includes many thousands of scientists and academics, by the way, and according to one source the number of creation-believing scientists grew from 700 in 1987 to some 24,990 in 1997.[12]

A Matter of Integrity

As mentioned at the outset, a number of books, articles, and websites I have visited attempt to use the Bible to defend the concept of animal rights. Most of these have come into being in the past few years, and virtually all of their arguments are highly flawed and based on my old personal supposition, which is common to all false religions: The Bible is full of errors except where it says what one wants it to say. It is oxymoronic for animal rights advocates to try to use the Bible to defend their position while discounting as inaccurate, archaic, or fanciful whatever portions don't fit their needs or with which they don't agree.

There are many extensive resources to prove that the inerrant Holy Bible has always been the same one generally accepted all around the world today, and that it has remained unchanged. There has seldom been any debate over which books should be included in the Hebrew version of the Old Testament. The first church "canon" (official meeting to decide which New Testament Scriptures were inspired by God and thus authoritative) was the Muratorian Canon of A.D. 170. The Muratorian Canon included all of the current New Testament books except Hebrews, James, and 3 John, which were added at the Council of Laodicea in A.D.

363. The Council of Hippo (A.D. 393) and the Council of Carthage (A.D. 397) both reaffirmed the same 27 books we have in the New Testament today as authoritative. Catholics added 12 of the 15 known books of the Apocrypha to their Bible at the Council of Trent in 1546. These writings, which were all done between 450 B.C. and the time of Christ, have always been recognized by the Church as important and useful but not authoritative or inspired by God. Jews consider them historical documents but not inspired, and they are not a part of the Hebrew Bible that we call the Old Testament. They certainly contain historical elements but often include obvious legend or fantasy, unlike the inspired books. For the interested person, innumerable resources are available to check for the accuracy of the Holy Scriptures, but these are far beyond the scope of this treatise.

For purposes of this book, I shall assume to be true what all the internal and external evidence strongly proves, and what my life experience has vindicated completely: The Holy Bible we hold in our hands today is completely free of error in the original texts, from the first word of Genesis to the last word of Revelation (the Apocrypha excluded). While I am no Hebrew or Greek scholar, I have studied the Scriptures to the extent that I am convinced that modern translations can usually be trusted to reflect the true intention of the original authors. We have available for analysis thousands of Biblical manuscripts in the original languages, from the Dead Sea scrolls containing the Old Testament to second-century copies of virtually all the New Testament. Overall we can count only one word in a thousand about which there is even any question as to its meaning, and no significant concept or doctrine is affected at all by this small number.

Using this essential premise of infallibility, we will first delve into the past and then into the future. Much of what is here could be new to you, so my advice is for you to ask God to help you sort it out. I believe it is as important to you as it has been to me, and that failing to recognize the truth of God's Word is a formula for living a frustrating life that leaves a person dissatisfied and unfulfilled, no matter how much worldly wealth or fame he accumulates.

Notes

1 www.icr.org/article/science-vs-scripture-open-response-dr-john-ankerbe [accessed March 2009].

2 The John Ankerberg Show, *Constituent Letter*, January 2009.

3 Daniel R. Brooks and E. O. Wiley, "Entropy: The Great Illusion," *Evolution*, Vol. 40, No. 4 (1986), 879–881.

4 Walt Brown, *In the Beginning: Compelling Evidence for Creation and the Flood*, 8th ed., www.creationscience.com.

5 George Caylor, "The Biologist," *The Ledger*, Vol. 2, Issue 48, No. 92, Dec. 1, 2000.

6 "The Disappearing USA," *Scientific American*, Vol. 211 (Oct. 1964), 58.

7 David N. Menton, PH.D., "There Ought to Be a Law Against Evolution—And There Is!" *St. Louis MetroVoice*, Sept. 1993, Vol. 3, No. 9.

8 Sir Fred Hoyle, *Mathematics of Evolution*, Acorn Enterprises, 1999.

9 www.mathematicsofevolution.com/ChaptersMath/Chapter_130 _Basic_Mathematics_.html [accessed February 2009].

10 Murray Eden, "Inadequacies as a Scientific Theory," *Mathematical Challenges to the Neo-Darwinian Interpretation of Evolution*, No. 5, Wistar Institute Press (1966), 11.

11 Gevin Giorbran and Devin Harris, "Omega Zero; The Influence of the Future on Cosmic Evolution, Part Two: Introducing Two Opposing Types of Order," March 3, 2004, www.cosmicsymmetry.com [accessed February 2009].

12 www.ridgecrest.ca.us/~do_while/sage/v5i1of.htm [accessed March 2009].

TWO

In the Beginning

The Deadly Assumption

I T is hoped that the previous chapter may give occasion for believers in evolution, from Christians to atheists, to reexamine their position in light of the verifiable hard evidence against this foolish theory. The foundation laid in that chapter calls into question numerous basic assumptions of evolution and the so-called evidence that backs them. This material is necessary to lay a foundation for this and the next chapter.

There is a fundamental and fatal flaw that permeates the overwhelming majority of our academic and scientific communities. Despite its demonstrable inaccuracy, this misleading assumption is increasingly the official state religion of most non-Muslim nations. The flaw is the notion that all things must, out of some kind of convoluted and vague necessity, be explained to exist and function without a Creator God. According to this worldview, the Biblical account of creation, the initial perfect world, man's fall from his original unblemished relationship to God, and the consequent necessity of the moral imperatives of the Bible as we know it today, all must be disbelieved and completely discounted. Here I want to review and attempt to clarify what many writers more talented than I have already done: I want to challenge this flaw with the logic of Holy Scripture.

At first glance this flaw may appear to have little or nothing to do with animal rights. In fact, however, it is *the* major key to understanding the whole concept of animal rights. Please bear with me while I attempt to lay a Biblical basis for this assertion.

Most people who read this book are probably already Christians of some stripe, but even if you happen to be an atheist, let me ask you to assume, only for the sake of illustration, that every part of the Bible is literally true, down to the very word. I would ask you to carry this assumption through at least the next two chapters, after which you are free to revert to your chosen position. Especially if you are a skeptic like I was, it is impossible to visualize what I'm talking about if you don't for a moment assume it's factually true.

If we reason that the Bible is perfectly true, most scholars would agree that the Biblical timeline allows only for a young Earth and a young universe. The Bible states that God created everything in the physical universe in a particular order in six literal days. The Hebrew text does not allow for these days to be otherwise, since everywhere else the word for "day" is used in the Bible, it means a literal 24-hour day. When God finished the work of creation, He proclaimed it "good," which, coming from God, could only mean "perfect." It is hard for today's secular mind to even conceive that "millions of years" haven't actually existed at all. As noted in the previous chapter where I quoted an unnamed molecular biologist, the dogma is strong and unyielding, and peer pressure to conform to this distorted thinking is incredibly brutal. Ridicule, ostracism, and worse await anyone who has the gall to even question the prevailing evolutionary creed, the total absence of evidence to support it notwithstanding. An academic who believes literally in the Biblical scenario, and lets it become public knowledge, might have a very hard time attaining tenure. A scientist might find it impossible to advance in his chosen field, whatever that might be, from astronomy to zoology. The scientific method must not be very important in either science or academia; one's personal belief system is apparently paramount.

What If It's Really True?

But I ask you for the moment to go against this rigidly enforced academic and scientific creed, open your eyes for a short time, and assume that in the beginning the world was created perfect by God. That being our hypothesis, let's try to describe what such a world might look like. Man would know God personally, and because man was created the physical world's only moral agent, he alone would have the capacity to disobey God. Man would live in a world where there existed perfect conditions for living and ideal growing conditions for plants and animals, literally from pole to pole.

Such a world, and how it functioned, is described in near-scientific terms in the early chapters of the Bible's book of Genesis. There are no fantastic scenarios painted in the Bible, such as a turtle crawling through space with the world on its back. None of the prevalent but erroneous Egyptian theories on the creation of the cosmos found their way into the Bible, either, even though this was the educational background of Moses, who recorded the events for us from oral, and possibly written, records. This evidence alone gives great credence to the Bible as being authoritative and accurate.

Considering only the evidence in the Bible, it becomes quickly apparent that the world was created essentially like a terrarium, with some degree of a transparent vapor canopy in the upper layers of the atmosphere. This canopy likely would not have been a significant factor in a future worldwide flood, apparently, due to heat problems if sufficient quantities of water had been present and had precipitated to create the flood.[1] A limited canopy nevertheless would have been adequate to block the majority of harmful cosmic and solar radiation, while allowing friendly sunlight, moonlight, and starlight to enter mostly unhindered. It also would spread the sun's heat evenly over the world, so Antarctica would have been as warm and productive as the equator. There would have been no extremes of temperature and only slight cooling at night. Some highly knowledgeable creationism scientists disagree with these statements to varying degrees, and I respect divergent opinions, but to me the Bible's clear indication of a perfect planet indicates there were no stressful conditions anywhere for plants, animals, or people in that world.

In a perfect atmosphere completely free of particles, there could have been no rain, since every raindrop, even today, must condense around a particle (the basis of "cloud seeding" to produce rain). The Bible explicitly states that in the original, perfect world, there was no rain, yet God made provision for all-inclusive irrigation even before He created plants and animals (Genesis 2:5). The system was designed to provide water to the creation when "a mist used to rise up and water the whole surface of the ground" (verse 6). This is exactly how plants are watered in a terrarium. Water condenses in very subtle fashion when temperature and humidity are ideal, to be reabsorbed and recycled by plants. The key to a successful terrarium, in fact, is that all conditions must be "perfect."

Another interesting possibility for this irrigation system has been offered: "This mist was not dew, for dew would not provide enough water to keep things alive, nor would it provide enough runoff to keep the four rivers outside the Garden of Eden flowing.... Some suggest that the mist came from a system of underground reservoirs called aquifers. The physical characteristics of these aquifers are not known. How the water was stored and how the aquifers were replenished is also unknown. We do know that the Bible says there was a mist robust enough to water the whole surface of the earth. The aquifers might have been a pressurized, world-wide sprinkling system with the pressure supplied by geothermal heat."[2]

This pressurized system of underground water could have played a huge role in supplying sufficient water to produce a worldwide flood. We will discuss this in more detail in the next chapter.

There is outstanding scientific evidence that God's original two human creations, Adam and Eve, are the father and mother of all mankind. To cite a science source relevant to Eve, mitochondrial DNA studies indicate that all people are descended from a single human female, and this individual has even been termed the "Mitochondrial Eve."[3] Mitochondrial DNA is inherited only from the mother, and it has been shown that every human being on earth originated with a single woman sometime in the past. Evolutionists believe this "mother of all the living" lived 200,000 years ago and that it is purely coincidental that all human lines diverge from her (Genesis 2:20). This cannot be so because mitochondrial DNA mutates rapidly and would have certainly changed had it been more than a few thousand years since this woman existed.[4, 5] As for Adam, y-chromosome studies (the y-chromosome is found only in males) have shown that the entire human race is also descended from a single man. Data also suggest a recent date for this "y-Chromosome Adam."[6] In both these instances, the Biblical record is solidly verified, despite attempts by orthodox evolutionists to minimize the significance of these findings.

Not Created Equal!

There is also a key point in the act of creation that should not be overlooked, even though it conflicts severely with today's evolutionary orthodoxy and with the animal rights movement as a whole. Even the Declaration of Independence of the United States of America acknowledges that all men were created equal in the sight of God; however, man and animals were *not* created equal. It is clearly stated that God created man in His own image, and that man was created to rule over the physical realm, including animals (Genesis 1:26-28). I will refer to man as God's image-bearer from time to time in this book. The uniqueness of man and his superiority to animals is reaffirmed in Genesis 9:6 in the prohibition against shedding the blood of fellow human beings, but not that of animals. This verse also forms the Biblical basis of capital punishment for the crime of murdering a fellow human being, an act that amounts to vandalizing the very image of God. This is restated in the Mosaic Law in Exodus 21:12, 34, where loss of an animal is to be recompensed with a like animal, but killing a man is reason for the death penalty.

A central figure in the Bible is King David, who ruled the nation of Israel for 40 years from approximately 1010 B.C. to 970 B.C. Despite some unfortunate defects in his personal life that are recorded in the Bible (another proof the Bible is true—even kings are presented with blemishes, warts, and all), he proved his reliance on God over and over in good times and bad, and God made several specific promises to him. His line would produce the eventual Messiah, and the genealogy of both earthly parents of Jesus Christ shows them to be descended from King David (Joseph in Matthew 1:1-17, and Mary in Luke 3:23-38).

David wrote much of the beautiful book of Psalms, and he affirmed repeatedly the awesome nature of the Creator God he served. He also appreciated the uniqueness of man and his diſtinct superiority to animals. He wrote of God and man in Psalm 8:3-8, "When I consider Your heavens, the works of Your fingers, the moon and the ſtars, which you have ordained; What is man that You do take thought of him? And the son of man that You care for him? Yet You have made him a little lower than God, And You have crowned him with glory and majeſty! You make him to rule over the works of Your hands; You have put all things under his feet, All sheep and oxen, And also the beaſts of the field, The birds of the heavens, and the fish of the sea, Whatever passes through the paths of the seas." Who can doubt that this inſpired writer knew well that man is God's image-bearer, created a superior being from the beginning, and not a higher, more evolved animal?

This well-defined concept is lived out through the whole Old Teſtament, and is reaffirmed by Jesus Chriſt Himself, and others, in the New Teſtament. (We will go into more detail in Chapters Eight and Nine). Chriſt clearly ſtates in Matthew 10:29-30 that a human being is "more valuable than many ſparrows." Neither does He in any way condemn or criticize the fact that "two ſparrows are sold for a cent," that being the market price for ſparrow meat in those days. In Matthew 12:12, Jesus implies that a man's life can't even be calculated in terms of how many sheep it is worth, either. Man's individual value is infinite to God because man is the only creature ſtamped with the image of the great Creator God who ſtrung out the galaxies and all they contain, put together the cell with its myriad organelles, and designed the DNA molecule and the incredibly complex mechanism for its replication. God has created man with awesome capabilities, and all of these reflect the genius of God Himself.

Neither man nor beaſt evolved to be vegetarians, or to become vegetarians; all were originally *created* as vegetarians by the hand of God (Genesis 1:29-30). Even dinosaurs of all kinds, as well as lions, tigers, ſpotted cats, bears, and hyenas, were created to eat green plants as food. That some were created with the *capacity* to eat other creatures is undeniable, even as man was created with the capacity to disobey God and the capacity to digeſt meat, but the Bible clearly proclaims that death—even animal death—entered the world through the disobedience of the physical world's only moral agent: Man.

It was not as if God had failed to warn Adam of the consequences of disobedience. There was only one rule in Eden: "From any tree in the garden you may eat freely; but from the tree of the knowledge of good and evil you shall not eat, for in the day that you eat from it you will surely die" (Genesis 2:16-17). Since Adam and Eve didn't die immediately on eating the fruit, we can assume that their spiritual death took place in the breaking of perfect fellowship with God, and that their bodies began to decay until they ultimately experienced physical death.

Disaster and Consequences in Eden

The Apostle Paul reaffirms this with great clarity in the New Testament when he states "Just as through one man sin entered the world, and death through sin" (Romans 5:12). Until man's sin, recorded as a scene in the Garden of Eden in Genesis 3:1-7, there was no death. It is obvious to me that this was true not only of man and higher animals, but also of insects and other lower life forms, as well as plants. It is quite evident that death was completely foreign to the perfect original creation.

After Adam's disobedience of God and the disastrous broken relationship, many things changed, but some aspects of the perfect creation persisted for a time. Many vital features, perhaps even most, stayed in place until the flood of Noah. Human death certainly entered the world when Cain, Adam's first son, killed Abel, his second (Genesis 4:2-8). It is interesting and informative to note that the murder was committed out of Cain's jealousy that his younger brother's sacrifice was affirmed by God as better than his own. The most remarkable aspect is the fact that Abel was commended for the righteous offering of *animal sacrifices*, an act that was obviously greatly pleasing to God. His rejection of Cain's vegetarian offering may simply reflect the man's attitude and spiritual condition, but it also foretells a Biblical principle that is later outlined clearly in the Law of Moses (perhaps most clearly in Exodus 24:8): The shedding of blood (and the resultant death) is necessary in order to restore fellowship with a holy God and to cover man's many acts of disobedience before Him. As Scripture states, "For the life of a creature is in the blood and I have given it to you to make atonement for yourselves on the altar; it is the blood that makes atonement for one's life.... The life of every creature is its blood" (Leviticus 17:11, 14). We later learn that the animal sacrifices of the Old Testament didn't fully pay for man's sin, but were only a picture of what was necessary: A perfect sacrifice to obtain perfect and lasting forgiveness. Jesus Christ's death on the cross is His death for my sin; it is a substitution so I don't have to die for my own sin, because He died in my place. Sacrifice of animal blood only "reminded" man about his sin; it didn't do away with it like Christ's sacrifice (Hebrews 10:3-4). This principle is clearly stated in an earlier chapter in that book of the New Testament, which says that "without shedding of blood there is no forgiveness" of sin (Hebrews 9:22).

Probably animal death began immediately after the fall of man. God had to take the lives of animals in order to clothe Adam and Eve (Genesis 3:21) when they suddenly understood, immediately following their act of sin, that they were naked. Many believe God obtained this skin for their clothing when he personally performed the first animal sacrifices in history to temporarily restore fellowship with his highest creation, His image-bearer. Adam and Eve covered their nakedness with fig leaves (plant material), but bloodshed—the only sufficient atonement—was necessary to "cover" their sin. Furthermore, the animals were killed by God's own hand to illustrate that He alone provides the remedy to our sin. Additionally, their son Abel offered animal sacrifices, so animal death must necessarily have been ongoing prior to any human death. Animal death, too, is thus ultimately a consequence of man's sin. Some few decades after Adam's sin, the Bible records the first human mortality when Cain killed Abel, making homicide the first cause of a human death.

Despite the advent of death as a phenomenon for the first time, the particle-free atmosphere, the irrigation system, and the critical water vapor canopy were still intact and functional. God had designed this perfect system in order to allow all creatures to live forever. Today, with every breath, a human being inhales a pint of air and takes in between 1 million and 300 million particles of matter, depending on whether they are in the middle of the Pacific Ocean or downtown in a big city.[7] Such massive doses of particles are clearly a major health risk to people and animals. Compared to the pristine pollution-free atmosphere that existed before the flood, the world's creatures today live in a virtual smoke-filled room.

Even though the effects of sin caused all physical bodies to begin a slow process of decay, in these near-perfect conditions man (and probably animals as well) lived to an awesome lifespan that today seems inconceivable, and even fanciful. Unfortunately, this long life had the unpleasant downside of making man feel immortal and act immorally on a scale probably not seen since (though I think we're getting close, except as to the seasoning effect of dedicated Christians—personal observation).

Huge relational changes paralleled the physical changes in the world after the advent of sin. Man's fellowship with God was broken, of course, but loss of his perfect relationship to animals was another casualty, since the death-free world was now lost. Man had been specifically given dominion over animals and, as noted in the case of Abel, he even tended domestic stock long before the flood. However, the flesh of these long-lived animals was apparently consumed infrequently by man, though there is no specific Biblical prohibition against doing so. In fact, the notation that Abel sacrificed animals (Genesis 4:4) strongly suggests that man did eat meat, with God's blessing, prior to the flood, since animal sacrifices were usually consumed, at least partially. Eating part of many animal sacrifices was specifically prescribed in the Law of Moses, which came hundreds of years after the flood, though such consumption was not necessary for human survival prior to the flood. Doubtless man also utilized animal skins for clothing, as evidenced by the fact that God personally clothed Adam and Eve in animal skins. Such necessary sacrifices and the need for clothing would also explain the utility of early herding of domestic stock after the fall, even without the eating of animal flesh. Perhaps man learned to utilize milk and other dairy products quite soon after the fall, as well.

There is other scriptural evidence that man ate animal flesh prior to the flood, probably as part of the holy ritual of sacrifice to God. Jabal (Genesis 4:20) is identified as the father of cattle keepers, so Abel's herding was no aberration. Additionally, God told Noah to take seven pairs of "clean animals" onto the ark, an order that could imply the need for eating their flesh after the flood. Since there is no positive prohibition against eating animals prior to the flood, it seems obvious that humans would have consumed animal flesh prior to the flood, at least for ceremonial purposes, if not also for nutrition and because they liked the flavor!

Human tooth structure is cited by vegetarians and by many scientists as evidence of man's vegetarian origins. We have no long, ripping incisors like a predator, but instead our front teeth seem designed for biting softer material such as fruit. Human molars are perfect for crushing plant material. Meat tends to lodge between our teeth to a greater degree than plant material, making cavities and gum disease more likely. These advocates are right, and some might be surprised to discover that the Bible is in perfect alignment with their position. Other body features of human beings, such as skin pores for dissipation of heat and the relative length of the digestive tract, are alleged to be more like those of vegetarian animals than those of carnivores. It seems highly probable that man, as well as most land animals, remained principally vegetarian until after the flood of Noah, another point that we will explore more in the next chapter.

Still, God supplied man (as well as certain other creatures) with all the tools necessary to utilize meat, including hydrochloric acid in the stomach and wonderful protein-cleaving enzymes in the pancreas. Neither of these would have been needed on a purely vegetarian diet, and indeed strict herbivores like sheep lack both these faculties, a discussion we will pursue in a later section (Chapter Ten).

Most of the original physical creation remained intact at this point, with the main changes being relational, along with the disastrous intrusion of death. All the original species created still lived together, perhaps in relative peace, on the earth. One thing appears certain: The unspoiled terrarium-like planet was still a great place to live, even after Adam's sin. Perfect growing conditions worldwide likely persisted through several centuries or millennia, with massive buildup of vegetative humus from falling leaves and—yes—dying plants.

God Deals With Depravity

As mentioned, man's long lifespan led to an indescribable level of depravity. When death may be hundreds of years away and aging is so slow it is barely detectable, it must have seemed an eternity to the grave and youthfulness probably appeared to have no end. Doubtless life in general was easy and good while personal accountability to God seemed very distant, assuming significant numbers of pre-flood people even held a belief in God. From reading the Genesis account of pre-flood society, one must assume that the faithful man, the one who sought and served God with all his heart, was the rare exception even then. We do know that by the time Noah and his eight-member family got aboard the ark, they were the only people on earth who believed in the one true God. Such a wicked, violence-filled world had arisen because of long lives and general disbelief, a situation that demanded action by God.

In preparation for the flood, God used Noah and his sons to build an immense boat to hold a pair (or, in some cases, seven pairs) of every land animal. The boat is described in the Bible as having three levels and being 450 feet long, 75 feet wide, and 45 feet high, dimensions that are the epitome of stability for a ship that size, a fact that is highly unlikely to be accidental. Whitcomb and Morris have noted in their book, *The Genesis Flood*, that such a colossal vessel's internal capacity would be equivalent to some 522 standard railroad boxcars, and it could easily hold 55,000 sheep-size animals, a good approximation of how many species of various sizes it would have to house in order to keep alive every basic kind of land animal in existence.

One should also consider that the original gene pool was exceedingly rich, and far fewer different kinds of animals could have adapted to new post-flood habitats to produce the numerous related species and subspecies we have today, meaning it might not take nearly all the available space on the ark to house all the created "kinds" that gave rise to the numerous varieties now in existence. It took Noah and his three sons one hundred years to complete the boat according to the specifications provided by God. On command from God, the designated animals came to the ark and entered it—Noah didn't have to do a roundup (Gen 7:15). That God was involved in gathering the animals is confirmed in the small bit of information stating "and the LORD closed" the door (Genesis 7:16). Once inside the ark, many animals probably slept most of the time, a trait we see today in the hibernation of some animals during periods of stress. Extremely large beasts were probably juveniles, much smaller than adults.

Assuming the Biblical account is correct, one can easily see how the fossils and fossil fuels were formed. Fossil formation requires rapid coverage of the subject by sediment after a creature's death, and only a universal flood could accomplish this on the massive scale we see all around today's world. Vast amounts of oil, coal, and natural gas resulted when thousands of years of continuous vigorous plant growth, its debris deposited worldwide on forest floors, resulted in continent-sized rafts which became waterlogged and sank to the bottom, where they were covered by a heavy overburden of sediment. Calculations have shown that the Biblical timeline is quite sufficient to account for the amount of fossil fuels present in the world.[8] This is especially so if one considers that the pre-flood world was ideal for plant productivity, the land mass may have been much larger than it is today, and there likely was no "down time" caused by any significant change of seasons. As well, there is plentiful evidence of a totally different extinct ecosystem of "floating forests" that were vast and productive.[9, 10] Such rapid burial of these organic graveyards would have been necessary to explain the chemical composition of these deposits, which have at least some common characteristics wherever in the world they are found. As a result of pressure from sedimentary overburden and deterioration of carbon-based humus in a low-oxygen environment, an incalculable volume of fossil fuel was produced with little loss to oxidation.

As noted, the Bible states unequivocally that there had never been rain before Noah entered the ark. There was a dormant source of particles to allow for rain, however. Not surprisingly, the Bible even has the events in the correct sequence: "[O]n the same day all the fountains of the great deep burst open [massive movement of the earth's crust and consequent worldwide volcanic eruptions, another first—brackets mine], and the floodgates of the sky were opened" (Genesis 7:11). When the water vapor canopy, however limited its extent, was blasted by innumerable microscopic particles, the first rain started to fall. This would not have been sustainable for the Biblical "forty days and forty nights," however, so volcanic activity associated with the breaking up of the earth's crust, both on land and in the oceans, could conceivably have "created a linear geyser (like a wall) of superheated steam from the ocean, causing intense global rain."[11] A pressurized irrigation system utilizing vast underground aquifers, as described earlier, could have been highly significant in this event. The hydroplate theory proposed by one prominent creation scientist appears to be very much a possibility.[12] In addition, this well-laid theory addresses and provides ready, logical answers to many otherwise-unanswerable questions about geological and astral phenomena.

Whatever the source or mechanism, the scriptural statement about the windows of heaven opening is an apt description of worldwide torrential rain. This raging downpour was like the world had never seen and will never see again. Forty days of constant deluge completely precipitated any protective canopy, while rapidly moving continental plates (or simple breakup and collapse of the earth's crust) created steam geysers that kept the downpour going as they released massive amounts of subterranean water. Every human being and every vertebrate land animal that was not aboard the ark perished. In a world characterized by very low mountains, or likely none at all in most locations, there was nowhere to escape except aboard the ark. Countless bodies eventually sank to the bottom, perhaps swirled into certain locations in greater numbers by eddies and currents. There, like the immense rafts of vegetation, they were quickly covered by copious sediments to form the fossils we know today.

The world was a completely different place half a year later, and that's what the next chapter is all about.

NOTES

1 L. Vardiman and K. Bousselot, "Sensitivity Studies in Vapor Canopy Temperature Profiles," Fourth International Conference on Creationism, August 3-8, 1998.

2 Kurt Howard, "Turbidites: A Challenge to Uniformatarianism," www.creationinthecrossfire.com/documents/turbidites, [accessed Feb. 2009].

3 *Nature Genetics*, 15:363-368, 1997, "Trends in Ecology and Evolution," 12(11):422-423, 1997; *Science*, 279 (5347):28-29, 1998; CEN *Technical Journal*, 12(1):1-3, 1998).

4 Christoph Richter, et al, "Normal Oxidative Damage to Mitochondrial and Nuclear DNA is Extensive," *Proc Natl Acad Sci USA*, Vol. 85, Sept. 1988, 6465-6467.

5 L. Loewe, et al, "Mitochondreal Eve: The Plot Thickens," *Trends in Ecology & Evolution*, Vol. 12, Nov. 1997, 422.

6 *Science*, 268 (5214):1183-85, May 26, 1995, 1141-1142.

7 www.projectrestore.com.library/health/pureair.htm, [accessed Feb. 2009].

8 G. Schöenknecht and S. Scherer, "Coal Deposits within the Geological Time-Scale," TJ *Archive*, 11(3):278-282, Dec. 1997.

9 C. Wieland, "Forests That Grew on Water," *Creation*, 18(1):20-24, 1996.

10 J. Scheven, "The Carboniferous Floating Forest—An Extinct Pre-flood Ecosystem," *CEN Technical Journal*, 10(1):70-81, 1996.

11 www.answersingenesis.org/home/area/tools/flood-waters.asp#f16, [accessed Feb. 2009].

12 Walt Brown, *In the Beginning: Compelling Evidence for Creation and the Flood*, 8th ed., www.creationscience.com.

THREE

A CHANGED WORLD

Cold, Wind, and Dust

WHEN Noah's ark finally came to rest on "the mountains of Ararat" (Genesis 8:4), the old prophet emerged to find a radically different environment. The unfamiliar sensation of cold at night was likely prominent long before the waters began to recede. The air must have choked the lungs of all the creatures on the ark, since none had ever inhaled any significant particulate matter. They perhaps felt something like a nonsmoker inhaling tobacco smoke. Compared to the pre-flood atmosphere, they were all now living as if in a dusty grain bin, a problem that would worsen as the barren, flood-soaked earth became drier and winds began to disperse surface dust and debris. A strong current of air in Noah's face must have seemed highly peculiar, too, since it was likely he had never felt more than a gentle breeze. We can make this assumption because the Bible never mentions weather until after the flood.

The first allusion to seasons and temperatures is in Genesis 8:22, where God tells Noah after his sacrifice of numerous animals, "While the earth remains, Seedtime and harvest, And cold and heat, And summer and winter, And day and night, Shall not cease." By this we can deduce that the cycle of the seasons likely did not exist before the flood.

For the waters to recede, significant geographical and topographical changes had to occur. For the available water to completely cover the highest mountains, those mountains of necessity could not have been more than a few thousand feet above sea level at most, and probably much lower. There could have been no Mount Everest or K2 (second highest mountain, part of the Karakoram segment of the Himalayan range) prior to the flood, if the Biblical record is accurate (as I'm asking you to assume for this and the previous chapter). Furthermore, for the waters to recede at all they had to have somewhere to go, so the seas must have been relatively shallow prior to the flood, leaving room for widespread sinking of the ocean floor. Water is moved by wind, by currents, and by seeking lower ground. The Bible clearly states that God set a final boundary for the sea (Proverbs 8:29; Psalm 104:8-9). It also plainly tells the mechanism by which today's vast mountain ranges, lofty and magnificent, were formed after the flood (Psalm 104:6-8).

As the waters receded and the mountains thrust upward, deep erosion of massive flood-generated sediments exposed worldwide layering in forming rock. Individual layers in rock appear to be caused by differential separation and deposition of sediments of differing weights as they are carried along by moving water and generally not by a single flood in a given year, which is what most evolutionary and other geologists maintain. Since a single layer in sedimentary rock is never (or almost never) caused by a single localized flood, observing the Grand Canyon and attributing its numerous layers to repeated local floods over millions of years may be scientifically indefensible. An indescribable volume of water running like a tide off the land and eroding layers *already created by shifting flood sediments* is a far more plausible explanation. Some creation scientists make a strong case for formation of the Grand Canyon some centuries after the Great Flood, since a significant degree of hardening of layered flood sediments would be necessary for the formations observed in the Desert Southwest of the USA today.

This hypothesis of layering by flood sediments is much more than idle speculation. The eruption of Mount St. Helens on May 18, 1980, was accompanied by glacial melting and consequent massive flooding. It also gave rise to huge volumes of local sediment, and post-eruption runoff cut through this newly-deposited material to expose myriad layers, much like those seen in the Grand Canyon.[1, 2] Interestingly, standard radioisotope decay studies have yielded an age for these new rocks in a fantastic range that approaches three million years, even though they were observed in formation in 1980.[3] It seems more than obvious that there is some important deficiency in the basic assumptions routinely applied in any radioisotope decay study designed to determine the age of rocks.

I believe that volcanic eruptions at the onset of the flood were the first movement of the earth's massive surface structure, or what geologists today refer to as "plate tectonics." The Bible tells us in Genesis 10:25 concerning the descendants of Noah, "and two sons were born to Eber; the name of the one was Peleg, for in his days the earth was divided." Of course, the majority of plate tectonics experts are convinced that this process has been going on very slowly for millions of years, but it seems much more logical to assume that such tectonics were highly accelerated during and immediately after the flood, resulting in the shifting and fragmentation of whole continents over a relatively short period of time. There is a far better hypothesis than standard, slow geological plate tectonics, however, in the much better explanation provided by the "rapid-onset hydroplate theory" of Dr. Walt Brown,[4] a former evolutionist who is a West Point graduate and holds a Ph.D. from the Massachusetts Institute of Technology, and was a tenured professor at the Air Force Academy. A full discussion of his likely explanation of earth's history, mechanics of the universal flood, and how it impacted the entire Solar system, is beyond the scope of this book, but those interested in more information are strongly encouraged to look to the referenced work.

This kind of sudden geological change would have led to drastic sinking of the sea floor accompanied by pushing upward of mountain ranges to previously unknown heights. It is undeniable that movement of the earth's plates, along with volcanism and minor mountain-building, is still occurring today. The scale, however, is quite minimal compared to what happened during and perhaps for some hundreds of years after the flood as the earth finally settled into an uneasy equilibrium.

Atmospheric conditions must have seemed awfully strange to Noah when he emerged from the ark. Whatever protective vapor canopy that existed previously had been ripped away, so there could no longer be even distribution of heat around the globe. As noted above in Genesis 8:22, the phenomenon of weather became known for the first time in history as the agitated atmosphere formed into swirling clouds, frontal systems, high and low pressure zones, and all manner of precipitation. The horrible trauma to the earth from the cataclysm may even have initiated the cyclic change in earth's orbit with respect to the sun, now 23½ degrees off perpendicular, resulting in changing seasons for the first time since creation. Of course, it is possible this orbital plane existed prior to the flood; nevertheless, no major change of seasons occurred before that event due to even heat distribution worldwide by the earth's theoretical vapor canopy.

The earth gave up a tremendous amount of heat energy due to events surrounding the flood, and worldwide volcanic eruptions surely obscured the sun significantly. The postulated super geysers at the beginning of the flood also could have continued for some years or more afterward, sending copious subterranean water high into the atmosphere, where it cooled and fell in intense blizzards of snow at higher latitudes. By one or all of these mechanisms, the Ice Age inevitably followed the great flood as a natural consequence. There doubtless was some ebb and flow of glaciers, but there was likely only one big ice event.

So much water became trapped in glaciers to be slowly released that quite a few animals that left the ark, or more likely their descendants, made it across the Bering Land Bridge into the Americas before the shallow Bering Sea refilled. Another possibility is that the floor of the Bering Sea, like sea floors worldwide, sank considerably over the first few centuries after the flood, eventually assuming its present depth. The retreat of glaciers, which began as the earth equilibrated, is ongoing today and still is not complete, as evidenced by hundreds of alarmist internet sites dedicated to the phenomenon. I would point out, however, that many glaciers have not retreated measurably, and in the Himalayas, where India alone has 9,575 glaciers, no retreat at all can be documented with certainty.[5] Moreover, any known glacial retreat could very well be only a continuing aftermath of the comparatively recent Ice Age, a possibility that is anathema to "global warming" advocates. Few of the internet sites have ironclad information going back further than a hundred years. How rapidly the glaciers retreated prior to that is not nearly as well documented and appears to be mainly conjecture but, overall, the rate of known glacial retreat certainly seems quite adequately explained in accordance with the Biblical timeline.

Animals from the ark moved in all directions into terrain particularly suited to their features and abilities. For example, very few wild sheep and goats migrated to Africa, with its flatter landscape, drier conditions, and paucity of open, high mountains and cliffs; species more suited to that habitat did so in large numbers.

It appears that while some animals migrated everywhere, the largest number of animal kinds gravitated toward Africa, which even today has by far the highest count of large animal species.[6] This could have been because of more favorable climate in that direction during the post-flood decades or centuries when great sheets of ice covered much of today's temperate zones. The animals that survived and prospered did so because whatever new habitat features they encountered were favorable to their continued existence and prosperity. It is an interesting fact that insect species (which could survive outside the ark as eggs) and plant species (surviving as seeds, spores, or root stock) are most numerous and varied in South America rather than Africa. One authority states, "Tropical South America is the most biodiverse region today."[7] South America has an estimated (although yet uncounted) two and a half million insect species, and in a single square kilometer up to seventy-five thousand species of trees and a hundred and fifty thousand kinds of higher plants can be found.[8] If evolution is true, it seems that one should expect these insect and plant species to be most numerous in Africa, the purported cradle of evolution, the same as with larger animals.

The Effect on Man

Man's environment was naturally changed drastically by the flood and its aftermath, as well. He was no longer shielded by the vapor canopy from cosmic and solar radiation, so harmful genetic mutations began to appear for the first time. Noah himself lived 350 years after the flood and died at age 950, personally immune to genetic mutations because these affect succeeding generations rather than current ones. Even ten generations after Noah, Abraham was able to marry his half-sister, Sarah, without any adverse genetic consequences (Genesis 20:12).

Adam and Eve's children married one another with impunity because they had perfect genes with no possibility of hereditary defects showing up in their offspring as a consequence of sibling unions. Doubtless, the idea of this kind of union being problematic never occurred to them. Today we have more than 4,500 known human genetic defects[9] and, contrary to evolutionary theory, not one of them improves the individual or their offspring. A search of the internet and the pertinent scientific literature turns up tons of pages dedicated to harmful genetic mutations. However, that much-touted beneficial Darwinian mutation is exceedingly elusive. The only instance ever to come to light, so far as I am aware, is the partial resistance of Africans with certain hemoglobin disorders to malaria. These would include sickle cell trait[10] and alpha thalassemia,[11] themselves serious diseases that make this hardly a positive tradeoff.

This is more evidence that runs counter to evolutionary theory, because had mankind been here for half a million years or more, we would have long ago been extinct from simple destruction of our genes. Marrying a relative, even a cousin, significantly increases the risk of genetic defects (up to twice as often as in unrelated couples) after several thousand years of cosmic bombardment. This is according to one respected journal which, paradoxically, made quite a splash by actually downplaying such risks.[12] Even among unrelated people who have children, the tragedy of genetic disease is all too frequent. That wasn't true in Abraham's day and, as noted, he actually married his half-sister. His son Isaac married Rebecca, a cousin, and Isaac's son Jacob also married two of his cousins. One should note that when Moses recorded the law hundreds of years after Abraham, however, he wrote into it without elaboration specific prohibitions against marrying close kin. Those additional several hundred years were enough to produce significant gene mutations, and certainly God was aware of that when He gave Moses the Law at Sinai.

The changed environment had many harsh effects. One was on man's longevity, which began to decline drastically after the flood, from 602 years for Noah's son Shem (who almost outlived Abraham), then 400+ years for the next three generations, then down to 175 years for Abraham, ten generations after the flood (Genesis 11:10-26; 25:7). No man after Abraham is recorded to have lived as long as 175 years, except for his son

Isaac, who lived to be 180 (Genesis 35:28), although it is certainly possible that other unrecorded men lived longer than these. Much of the decline in average age could probably be attributed to the newly particle-laden atmosphere, but some of it could be related to the change in food quality, plus the cumulative effects of cosmic radiation.

The Effect on Animals

Another consequence of the unforgiving new environment was extinction for those species unable to cope with changed conditions. Some dinosaurs quite apparently survived into medieval times as actual fire-breathing dragons, since there are numerous accounts, some quite reliable, of such giant reptiles up to that time in many parts of both the Old and New Worlds.[13] To quote the referenced book on one incident (out of more than 80 reports from Britain alone) that is alleged to have occurred in A.D. 1405 (page 60), "Close to the town of Bures, near Sudbury, there has lately appeared, to the great hurt of the countryside, a dragon, vast in body, with a crested head, teeth like a saw, and a tail, extending to an enormous length. Having slaughtered the shepherd of a flock, it devoured many sheep. There came forth in order to shoot at him with arrows the workmen of the lord on whose estate he had concealed himself, being Sir Richard de Waldegrave, Knight; but the dragon's body, although struck by the archers, remained unhurt, for the arrows bounced off his back as if it were iron or hard rock. Those arrows that fell upon the spine of his back gave out as they struck it a ringing of tinkling sound, just as if they had hit a brazen plate, and then flew away off by reason of the hide of this great beast being impenetrable. Thereupon, in order to destroy him, all the country people around were summoned. But when the dragon saw that he was again about to be assailed with arrows, he fled into a marsh or mere [Saxon, *a pool, lake, or the sea.*] and there hid himself among the long reeds, and was no more seen."

Such references are easy to find, too numerous to catalog exhaustively, and come from virtually every culture and people group. The similarity of these creatures to dinosaurs found in the fossil record is striking, especially since dinosaurs were unknown until their remains were first described centuries later by William Buckland in 1819. The cited reference, plus many others, refers to living dinosaur-like creatures predating Buckland by several centuries.

Mostly the great reptiles and amphibians died out for lack of adequate lush foliage for food, inability to survive cold temperatures, and perhaps other factors, such as changed feeding habits of other creatures, as I'll cover below. Smaller reptiles and amphibians were better able to adapt and survive.

Strong scientific evidence that dinosaurs lived just a few thousand years ago surfaced recently with the discovery of soft tissue (blood vessels, protein, and DNA fragments) in the femur of a female *Tyrannosaurus rex* found fossilized in Montana, structures that could never have survived intact for millions of years.[14] As expected, despite the obvious impossibility of such structures staying constant for so long, as well as more credible young-earth explanations, most non-creationist announcements of the discovery date the animal at 68 million years old. Also not surprisingly, research now turns to finding an explanation for how such fragile structures could survive so long, and not to an eminently more logical quest for a plausible alternative, since that might undermine or depreciate the blindly accepted evolutionary timeline. Even a carbon-14 study has apparently not been contemplated, since it is accurate only for formerly living material less than 6,000 years old, and would be of zero value on a specimen presumed to be 68 million years old. My prediction is that such a study would reveal an astonishing age of about 4,000 years for the subject T-rex, and that it would be accurate!

Before the flood, man's dominion over the animal kingdom was apparently absolute, but afterward that dominion was forever tarnished. If the relationship between man and animals had been previously respectful and cordial, God knew that would change drastically in view of new environmental and dietary realities.

New Dietary Realities

Every human being and every animal that walked, flew, or crawled off Noah's ark had a brand-new set of nutritional needs about which they could not be aware. A major unseen need was for cyanocobalamin, or vitamin B12, the most complex of the family of substances known as vitamins. It is not only the most complicated chemically, but its production, absorption, and availability to the body are also quite difficult to comprehend even today. The eight people and many of the animals leaving the ark also encountered a new difficulty in obtaining certain of the amino acids, particularly lysine and methionine, irreplaceable building blocks of protein. Some minerals, such as zinc, calcium, and iron, were also difficult to obtain from purely plant sources. Before the flood, all these were apparently obtained easily by human beings and all animals through eating green plants. After the flood, that was no longer the case, for reasons we do not fully understand. Either the plant (or plants) containing these nutrients perished in the flood, or else the ability of that plant (or maybe plants in general) to provide them was somehow destroyed by the flood. Perhaps the intrusion of intensified cosmic and solar radiation destroyed this avenue of production. In our post-flood world, only microorganisms are able to manufacture vitamin B12, and most that is available for use by higher animals and man is produced in the digestive tract of certain animals, where such bacteria are plentiful.

Whatever the case, animals fell into two categories as they disembarked from the ark: One category had adequate intestinal bacteria to provide its own intrinsic vitamin B12, and the ability to absorb and store it; the other lacked these faculties. This latter category necessarily was required to obtain this nutrient by eating the flesh of those animals whose intestinal bacteria provided it for them, though this quite obviously was not an intentional discovery. There may have been some residual ability in plants to produce vitamin B12 for a time, but eventually the need for this ingredient drove those animals that couldn't produce it to carnivorous activity. I think a delay in onset of carnivorous activity might have been likely, since prey species had to have time to reproduce and attain sufficient numbers to support a wide variety of animals we today call predators. Vitamin B12 is a long-lasting nutrient that is stored in high quantities in both animal and human tissues, so a significant deficiency in predators and humans could have been many months, or even a few years, in manifesting itself.[15] Human beings fall firmly into this latter category of creatures, although they were told clearly by God of His permission to eat animal flesh.

It is known that some vitamin B12 is produced in the human intestines, but most of it is unusable because it is manufactured in the colon and is unavailable to a human being without going through some rather wild and eminently modern gyrations. Since vitamin B12 is unavailable to people from any non-animal source, most human vegetarians get it from the smallest possible animal, either bacterial cultures or yeast. In the case of vegetarians who aren't all that strict about avoiding every animal product in their diet, vitamin B12 can be readily obtained in sufficient quantity from eggs and dairy products, as can most other nutrients that are hard to obtain purely from plant sources.

New Relational Realities

God made two astounding statements to Noah and his sons after they left their lifeboat. First, in Genesis 9:2, He told them that there was going to be a complete change in their longstanding relationship to animals. It was going to be harder for man, without weapons of any kind, to survive in the post-flood, dog-eat-dog world. The new reality was that eating the flesh of other creatures was now, or very soon would be, a biological necessity for predators, and without special protection man himself would surely become a prey species. God told Noah that He was going to put a terror of man on every animal on earth, including land animals, birds, and even the fish of the sea. This was God's safeguard for man, His highest creation and His image-bearer, and it is still in effect today. Even the biggest bears still almost invariably run headlong in the opposite direction at the slightest hint of man's scent, a fact I have personally witnessed many times.

This terror is absolutely illogical if evolution were true, because man has always been mostly helpless when confronting lions, tigers, bears, and other more powerful creatures. Even with the advent of modern firearms over the past couple of hundred years, these animals (meaning those which survive today) can still be daunting when encountered in the field. It doesn't necessarily require large size for an animal to be dangerous to people, either. Baboons, chimpanzees, and small cats are capable of doing considerable damage to a human being's tender flesh, although their God-instilled fear of man usually prevents this in the wild unless they are cornered, injured, or ill. (I listed chimpanzees here in my original manuscript almost a year ago, but even while I review this, news of an awful attack by a domesticated chimpanzee just came over the news, whereby the animal ripped off a woman's face, ate off most of her hands, and attacked police who came to her rescue. She is currently fighting for her very life.[16])

I will have more to say about this God-imposed fear of man by animals in later chapters because there are Biblical indications that it will be removed from animals as part of the coming apocalypse. Increasing numbers of unexpected attacks by many different kinds of predators on human beings are but a harbinger of terrible, terrifying times to come. We will go into this in detail at the appropriate point.

More on the Post-Flood Diet

The second statement made by God, the ultimate biochemist, was that He now "gives" mankind the flesh of any animal for food, so long as the blood is drained from it (Genesis 9:3). God obviously was totally aware that, along with the vapor canopy and perfect worldwide living conditions, the unmentioned vitamin B12 plant had been destroyed (or perhaps it was so compromised He knew it was headed for extinction). He also knew there were other dietary needs obtainable only from animal flesh. Eating meat was not abruptly endorsed because a juicy grilled steak tasted good; it was endorsed because God knew man could not survive without it. Animals also acted as efficient collectors and processors of unique and necessary nutrients no longer easily available, even laboring under the curse of the soil imposed in Genesis 3:17-19.

By using what most sensible people would term rather extreme means, including the latest scientific analyses of what nutrient can be found where, people living in our modern world can survive and do fairly well without meat. However, until very recently, before such facts as vitamins and amino acids, spirulina (blue-green algae extract), and bacteria were even remotely known, consuming meat was the only way to survive.

For most people in today's world outside temperate North America and Western Europe, meat is still the only way to survive and get the needed vitamin B12 and other key nutrients that are found richly only in animal flesh or animal products. And while a strict vegetarian (vegan) diet is difficult at best, an all-meat diet has been demonstrated to be exceedingly viable and healthful, with low rates of cancer and bowel disease being found in cultures that eat *only* meat.[17, 18] In fact, such findings absolutely contradict the dubious theory that an all-plant diet is healthful when one considers that vegans must give total concentration to their diet, or else they constantly teeter on the brink of malnutrition. It is also a fact that strict vegetarians in many societies live shorter lives. We will explore this topic in more detail in Chapter Ten.

The Bible Predicted It!

Rejection of the two central, critical truths in this chapter and the preceding one was predicted by the apostle Peter almost two thousand years ago in 2 Peter 3:3-6, where he states, "Know this first of all, that in the last days mockers will come with their mocking, following after their own lusts, and saying 'Where is the promise of His coming? For ever since the fathers [died], all continues just as it was from the beginning of creation.' For when they maintain this, it escapes their notice that by the word of God the heavens existed long ago and the earth was formed out of water and by water, through which the world at that time was destroyed, being flooded with water." Evolutionists blithely state, "In the beginning, hydrogen...." The Bible states, in effect, "In the beginning, di-hydrogen oxide (water)...."

To clarify, this passage as a whole is an unambiguous statement that eventually some men who are mockers will reject two of the most important foundational principles of God's Word and by this error go greatly astray. Those two principles are (1) God created everything in a short period of time by speaking the creation into existence; and (2) the great flood of Noah, resulting from the fall of man, destroyed the original perfect world and created the fossils along with myriad geological miracles and set in motion the world in which we live today. We are already seeing this prophecy fulfilled quite resolutely. Today there is absolute denial of both these ancient facts in the eminently successful promotion of the religion of evolution. The rise of the animal rights and radical environmental movements is the natural consequence, as these two ancient facts are carelessly dismissed as myth or error. The word "mockers" in this passage could also mean "scoffers," and that is exactly how the world at large views these two keystones of Biblical truth.

Along these lines, it would be remiss not to point out the next verse which states "But the present heavens and earth by His word are being reserved for fire, kept for the day of judgment and destruction of ungodly men" (2 Peter 3:7). It goes on to say in verse 10, "But the day of the Lord will come like a thief, in which the heavens will pass away with a roar and the elements will be destroyed with intense heat, and the earth and its works will be burned up." Hebrews 1:10-12 reaffirms this principle in quoting Psalm 102:25-26, stating that, "You, Lord, in the beginning laid the foundation of the earth, and the heavens are the works of your hands; they will perish, but you remain; and they all will become old like a garment, and like a mantle you will roll them up; like a garment they will also be changed but you are the same, and your years will not come to an end."

The whole premise of the radical environmental movement, as well as evolution and animal rights, is that the world, and, indeed, the whole creation, are practically eternal and that we therefore must do everything possible to make them last forever. By this they justify all manner of drastic changes in the way we live, and the unfortunate aspect is that even some Christians are taken in and deceived by their arguments; (I would point out one well-known Christian leader recently making commercials urging that we join the secularists in combating so-called "global warming"). The truth is that since the fall of man into rebellion against God, the earth's days have been numbered, no matter what we do to "save" the planet and its ecosystems. I am deeply in favor of managing the planet well, of being a good steward of all our resources and of taking reasonable and prudent steps to protect it. I am not willing to take radical steps to accomplish this, however, knowing that God is going to re-create the place we live so that it finally is perfect once more. Nor am I willing to concede that man is just another animal, and thus has no more rights than "creatures of instinct to be captured and killed" (2 Peter 2:12).

Make no mistake, the human population as a whole still can't survive without animal products, an idea radical animal rights proponents reject out of hand. When the apocalypse comes, this fact will be of infinite value to the Antichrist as he carries out his program to "improve" the world by means of fanatical human population control. A few undernourished, sometimes short-lived vegetarians are just a foreshadowing of that terrible time to come, a tragedy which is actually predicted specifically in the Bible. We'll also cover this aspect more thoroughly in Chapter Twelve. Post-flood vegetarianism was not God's intention, as evidenced by His own Word. It is exceedingly aberrant and a very recent phenomenon, or else by its widespread practice the human race could easily have been extinct long ago.

NOTES

1 H. A. Makse, et al, 1997, "Spontaneous Stratification in Granular Mixtures," *Nature*, 386:379-382.

2 J. Fineberg, 1997, "From Cinderella's Dilemma to Rock Slides," *Nature*, 386:323-324.

3 Stephen A. Austin, "Excess Argon within Mineral Concentrates from the New Dacite Lava Dome at the Mount St. Helens Volcano," *Creation Ex Nihilo Technical Journal*, 10(3):335-343, December 1996.

4 Walt Brown, *In the Beginning*, Part II, Center for Scientific Creationism, Eighth ed., 2008, 102-131.

5 Suarov Chakraborty, "Experts Debunk Glacial Retreat Theory," *Hindustan Times*, www.suaravrajaryan.blogspot.com, March 6, 2007.

6 Safari Club International's *Record Book of Trophy Animals*, Edition Ten.

7 Peter Wilf, quoted in "Fossils Show Extreme Plant Diversity in South America 50 Million Years Ago," *Science Daily*, April 4, 2003.

8 www.world66.com/southamerica, [accessed February 2009].

9 Jeffrey Steinberg, M.D., Fertility Institutes of Los Angeles, quoted from "The O'Reilly Factor," Fox News Network, March 2, 2009.

10 J. Carlson, et al, "Natural Protection Against Plasmodium Falciparum Malaria due to Impaired Rosette Formation," *Blood*, 1997, 84:3909-3914.

11 J. Flint, et al, "High Frequencies of Alpha-Thalassemia Are the Result of Natural Selection by Malaria," *Nature*, 1986, 321:744-750.

12 A. Motulsky, et al, "Genetic Counseling and Screening of Consanguinous Couples and Their Offspring," *Journal of Genetic Counseling*, 11:2, April 2002.

13 J. Simpson, *British Dragons*, B. T. Batsford Ltd., London, 1980.

14 Mary Schweitzer, "NC State Paleontologist Discovers Soft Tissue in Dinosaur Bones," *ScienceDaily*, March 25, 2005.

15 Z. Schneider and A. Stroinski, 1987, *Comprehensive B12: Chemistry, Biochemistry, Nutrition, Ecology, Medicine*, 199.

16 CNN Headline News, *Evening Edition*, Feb. 19, 2009.

17 Vilhjalmur Stefansson, "Eskimos Prove All-Meat Diet Provides Excellent Health," *Harper's Monthly*, November 1935.

18 Centre Hospitalier Universitaire de Quebec, Laval University, and University of Geulph, "Traditional Inuit Diet Cuts Heart Disease Risk," *American Journal of Clinical Nutrition*, Oct. 2001.

FOUR

POST-FLOOD
ANIMAL UTILIZATION

OKAY, now you're free to return if you wish to your atheist, agnostic, God-directed-evolution or skeptic position, if that's your philosophy. However, it would be helpful to your understanding of what I'm saying if you could continue to assume the Bible at least *could be* word-for-word accurate throughout because, for the next several chapters, the material is well-documented and not as controversial.

God *Likes* for Man to Use Animals!

A great deal of time passed, perhaps as much as a thousand years, between the flood of Noah and the giving of the Mosaic Law by God. Animals were used, with God's blessing and even His participation, over and over and in diverse ways during this interim. I will now touch upon some of those instances and then I'll try to draw some conclusions.

The first formal sacrifice of animals after the flood was made by Noah, who sacrificed one of each species of "clean" animals (mainly hoofed animals that ruminate their food, as well as some birds) as soon as they all left the ark (Genesis 8:20-21). This was a significant sacrifice of possibly a *hundred* animals or more. Moreover, it was a sacrifice that was highly pleasing to God, since there were only seven pairs of these animals left in the world. (It's a good thing there was no Endangered Species Act and no bureaucrats to enforce it back then!) Not only did

God realize that Noah and his family would need meat, but many now-predatory or soon-to-be predatory animals would, in due time, find it necessary to take some of these "clean" animals as prey. It was a great act of faith for Noah to sacrifice to God even one of these rare and precious creatures. Noah almost certainly sacrificed a male of each species, which would have had virtually no impact on reproduction (by the way, in the same way taking a male game animal in a sport hunt practically never adversely affects the ability of an animal population to thrive—and actually enhances the population in most instances by reducing sometimes-deadly competition for available females). The two main points that come from this episode are first, that God approves of the sacrifice and use of animals, and second, He obviously likes the aroma of animal flesh cooking ("A soothing aroma to the Lord"—I always think of a succulent steak sizzling on the grill, or the smell of a tender roast in the oven when I read this passage).

Immediately after this sacrifice, God made an unusual covenant with Noah and his sons to the effect that he would never again destroy the world by water (Genesis 9:9-17). The extraordinary aspect is that this covenant was between God and all living creatures, the only covenant in the Bible (and there are many) that includes creatures besides man as co-beneficiaries. God knew well that the wickedness and unbelief of man had led to widespread destruction of innocent animals, and I believe that is why he made this unique covenant with them, too. He set the rainbow in the sky as a reminder of that covenant, and He has been faithful to honor it. That first rainbow seen by Noah and his family was surely the first rainbow in history, since there had never before been rainfall to diffract light into its component colors prior to the flood.

Interestingly, the next reference to animal utilization involves not sacrifice or herding, but hunting (Genesis 10:8-12). Nimrod, a great-grandson of Noah, is twice described as "a mighty hunter before the Lord." There is no hint of condemnation of his hunting, but rather the spirit of the passage seems to be that Nimrod was a believing hunter who enjoyed God's blessing and approval. Some writers do attribute to Nimrod the rebellion against God at the Tower of Babel, where God supernaturally created all the diverse forms of human language in order to disunite and disseminate the human race, but evidence for this is indirect. It appears to me that, had Nimrod been involved in that occurrence, he surely would have been named in the account. Whatever his involvement, apart from such a supernatural event as occurred at Babel, the broad spectrum of different kinds of speech in the world is practically inexplicable. This is all the more so to the evolutionists in view of the relatively short period of time postulated by them since the "mitochondrial Eve" and "y-chromosome" Adam—between 100 and 200 thousand years.

This point is somewhat divergent from the main thrust of this book, but I include it because it adds credence to the veracity of ancient inspired Scripture. There are more than 6,500 distinct human languages,[1] though the majority of them are nearly extinct. The extreme variation and lack of commonality between them is both staggering and baffling to the evolutionist. If evolution is true, it appears that groups of human beings went off and developed their own language independent of the rest of mankind. As one authority has said, "One would be hard-pressed to come up with an example less amenable to evolutionary study. It's so chaotic it's like weather forecasting. The noise overwhelms the signal. There are some things in science that are very interesting, but that we're never going to be able to find out about. It's a sort of romantic view some people have, that anything interesting can be understood. If you can't define what it is, why study it from an evolutionary point of view?"[2] So much for the evolution of human speech. The Tower of Babel scenario is far more logical than language evolution, and far more plausible.

Herding of domestic stock occurred before the flood, and if certain domestic animals are descended from wild stock (and DNA studies suggest this in some cases[3]), then it seems fair to assume that some selective breeding occurred early in man's existence prior to the flood. This must be true because cattle are mentioned in the curse on the serpent after the fall (Genesis 3:14), as well as in the account of the flood, where cattle are specifically mentioned as being on the ark (Genesis 7:14, 8:1). Selective breeding of livestock (as well as pets) has no doubt been going on for thousands of years.

Abraham is the father of both Jews and Arabs, and later in his life he became heavily involved with livestock. He came originally from Ur, near Babylon, and went with his father and family to Haran (Genesis 11:31), far to the north of the land that became Israel, in present-day Turkey not far from the border with Syria. His father Terah died there, and God called Abraham to what we today call "the Promised Land," also known as Canaan (Genesis 12:1-4). In all these moves many possessions are mentioned, but no livestock. Abraham may have obtained his first livestock while visiting Egypt, when Pharaoh gave him gifts of sheep, cattle, donkeys, and camels (Genesis 12:16). He then proceeded to become a very rich herder and the owner of all sorts of livestock (Genesis 13:2).

Why Sacrifice?

Primarily, pre-Christian people sacrificed animals because God demanded it. The first direct, God-given command to sacrifice animals, as far as the Bible records, came when the covenant was made between God and the childless, elderly Abraham to make his descendants as numerous as the stars, and to someday give to his offspring the Promised Land (Genesis 15). God ordered Abraham to present a heifer (female of the cattle family), a goat, and a ram, all perfect specimens three years old, plus a dove and a young pigeon. In a rather bizarre ceremony, Abraham was to split the larger animals into halves, but not the birds. God, in blazing glory, passed between the sacrifices that night and sealed his promise to Abraham to eventually give his descendants all the land between the Euphrates and Nile rivers. By passing between the carcasses while Abraham was deep in slumber (15:12), God took upon Himself sole responsibility to be faithful to His promise to Abraham.

Abraham was certainly no stranger to red meat and animal products. In Genesis 18, he entertained three supernatural visitors. One was God Himself, likely in the person of the pre-incarnate Christ, because only two angels are mentioned as showing up to destroy Sodom and Gomorrah in the first verse of the next chapter. Moreover, the third individual is specifically identified as YHWH (the Hebrew proper name of God Almighty) ten times in Genesis 18, and as *Adonai* (Master, or Lord) five times. When Abraham saw the visitors, he recognized immediately that they were somebody special, even though they had assumed the appearances of men. He quickly and gladly offered them every kind of hospitality at his disposal. He had his wife begin making fresh bread while he ran and killed a calf to feed them. He also prepared fresh curds and milk. Verse 8 of this passage records irrefutably that *these supernatural beings ate red meat* plus curds and milk! And one of them was clearly God the Creator in human form.

Herding and livestock were a strong tradition with ancient Semitic peoples, even as they are a continuing occupation for millions today. Herding and keeping livestock are integral parts of the Bible story, too, and this fact is obvious even to the casual reader. A man's livestock was perhaps the main measure of his wealth, much as horses are still the measure of worth in places such as Mongolia, even in the present era. Most livestock was used for food, clothing, milk, and as beasts of burden. The most compelling reason to have livestock, however, was for sacrifice to God as a temporary covering for man's sins.

One particularly poignant example of such sacrifice occurred when God commanded Abraham to offer on an altar, Isaac, his only son by his wife Sarah (Genesis 22:1-17). Abraham was naturally quite stunned at such a radical directive from God, but he complied, some believe because he was so certain God could raise Isaac from the dead. He was stopped just short of killing his son when God supplied a ram, its horns caught in the bushes, as a substitute for Isaac. This passage also holds one of the earliest references to a coming Messiah who would be Abraham's descendant, and through whom "all the nations of the earth shall be blessed." In fact, the whole episode presents a beautiful foreshadowing of what God would actually do some two thousand years later in the provision of His only son as the requisite sacrifice for mankind's sin, even to the point of having Isaac carry the wood for burning the sacrifice, similar to the way Christ was compelled to carry his own wooden cross. God here gives us a glimpse of His intention to provide a greater and better sacrifice, a perfect sacrifice of His only Son, as full payment for man's sins.

Sacrificial procedures were not codified until the time of Moses, some seven hundred years later, but the need to practice animal sacrifice seems to have been pervasive among believers in the one true God, although it was also practiced by many pagans as well. Such sacrifices are still performed today, in fact. On a recent hunting trip to Nepal, I witnessed the sacrifice of a rooster to "the hunting gods" before we went out seeking mountain game. I let my Sherpa guides know that my personal sacrifice occurred two thousand years ago and that they should let the rooster live or else put him in the pot! Of course they did neither. Animal sacrifice is still the heart of the Jewish religion, though they have not had a temple in which to regularly fulfill this aspect of the Mosaic Law since the Romans destroyed Herod's temple and the city of Jerusalem in A.D. 70, as Christ had predicted shortly before (Mark 13:2). There is much to indicate that the reinstitution of animal sacrifices could play a major role in unleashing the wrath of the Antichrist on the nation of Israel if and when they do rebuild their temple, as some Bible scholars believe they will. As things currently stand, even sacrifice of the required lamb is usually suspended in the annual Passover commemoration.

Many, Many Uses for Animals

In myriad incidents in the Bible, livestock plays some part, such as when Abraham sent his servant to find a wife for his son Isaac, accompanied by a caravan of ten camels (Genesis 24:10). The servant explained Abraham's wealth to the girl's family (close relatives of Abraham, in fact) mainly in terms of his vast livestock holdings (Genesis 24:35). There are many more examples in the New Testament as well, and we will cover some in succeeding chapters.

There is a distinctly adversarial relationship in the Bible between man and wild beasts, already mentioned in the case of Nimrod the hunter. Esau, one of Isaac's twin sons, was his father's favorite and a skilled hunter (Genesis 27:3-5). Esau had his faults, such as presumptuously selling his birthright for a single meal (Genesis 25:33), and wanting to kill his brother Jacob after he tricked their father Isaac into giving him the blessing designated for Esau as the oldest son—a punishment that Jacob may have deserved (Genesis 27). However, none of Esau's faults relate to his hunting. In fact, he became a great man for his time, the father of the once-mighty nation of Edom. Moreover, he and his brother Jacob were apparently reconciled to some degree twenty years after they parted (Genesis 33:4). Much later, the judge Samson killed a lion with his bare hands (Judges 14:5-6). David did the same as a shepherd boy, killing both a lion and a bear when they attacked his flock (1 Samuel 17:36). One of King David's "mighty men," Benaiah, killed a lion as well (2 Samuel 23:20).

Some degree of antagonistic relationship is implied in the beginning by God's command to Adam to rule over and "subdue" the earth (Genesis 1:26-28). To "subdue" also means to be a good and wise steward, to utilize in sustainable fashion or conserve so we are not stealing resources from future generations. Biblical conservation has never meant total, untouchable preservation of any resource. However, there are examples, one of which is covered below, where outright elimination of a problem animal from man's proximity was Biblically indicated. In the usual sense, however, man's God-ordained dominion over the creation is essentially man's investment by faith of his time and energy in his possessions and his environment in order to add value to both. Even education, in this sense, is an investment by faith that adds value to an individual.

While it did not apply until after the flood of Noah, an important facet of subjugation of the creation has since been control of predators, a normal thing to do until very recent times, making the land safe for both livestock and people. In fact, God told the Israelites under Joshua, after the Egyptian bondage and liberation, and after their invasion of the Promised Land, that He would not allow them to conquer the whole region at once (Exodus 23:29). If He did, wild beasts (read: predators) might retake land from which they had already been extirpated before it could be firmly established under Israelite control.

Solomon, the wisest man to ever live, is featured prominently in animal stewardship. He obviously had no problem with animal utilization. He owned forty thousand chariot horses (1 Kings 4:26), and his daily provision of meat for himself and his administration was "ten fattened oxen [penned up and grain-fed, like we do today—brackets mine], twenty pasture-fed oxen, one hundred sheep in addition to deer, gazelles, roebucks, and fattened fowl" (1 Kings 4:22-23). Solomon obviously was God's man for the time, and he clearly was committed to utilization of animals as food and in other ways.

It is significant to me that three of the last four animals mentioned in this passage could be taken only by hunters. Solomon obviously appreciated the taste of wild game and the skill of the hunters he employed to secure it. Remember, the animals mentioned are wary and in those days the most advanced weapon to take them was the bow and arrow. Solomon even states in his writing, much of which is preserved as the Bible's Book of Proverbs (12:27), that the "lazy man does not roast his prey, but the precious possession of a man is diligence." In other words, one type of man wastes what he has killed in hunting, but the better man utilizes the animals. Solomon must have considered the skilled hunter who killed with a useful purpose to be sanctioned by God.

The prophetic books also include animal utilization as an accepted practice. In Isaiah 25:6, it states: "The LORD of hosts [God—brackets mine] will prepare a lavish banquet for all peoples on this mountain; A banquet of aged wine, choice pieces [of meat—brackets mine] with marrow." This appears to be evidence that we will still be meat eaters when the Kingdom of God is fully established on the new earth. Later I will present additional Biblical evidence that this could indeed be the case.

They're Back!

In Chapter Twelve, I also will have much more to say about the resurgence of predators in our modern world, which I liken to putting rats back into the barn or cockroaches back into the kitchen after first eliminating them. At public hearings across our nation in particular, the lack of concern for prey species, especially by *leaders* of the animal rights movement, is striking. Any game department's proposal to reduce prey species populations (elk, deer, and the like) is seldom met with any significant opposition such as lawsuits; however, let any increase in wolf control or the hunting of bear or cougar or anything else related to killing large predators come up, and there is a huge outcry—and it is usually highly organized, effectively vocal, and often involves legal action. As I write this, radical environmental and animal rights groups are seeking a court injunction to prohibit killing wolves outside Yellowstone National Park, where they were reintroduced a decade ago.[4] It was originally agreed that the three adjacent states would have a free hand to manage these efficient predators, which have already proliferated to some 1,500 animals outside Yellowstone. Not surprisingly, now these radical groups insist that at least 5,000 wolves are needed before any efforts are made to control their numbers. I can predict with great confidence that when this number is reached—which will probably occur before this book even goes to press—they will probably then push for 10,000 or more. There seems to be no end to the animal rights movement's appetite to protect large animals that can kill.

This predator favoritism and widespread carnivore restocking is not accidental. It is an integral and important part of a developing apocalyptic scenario, and it is fanatically urged on by the animal rights movement. The tragic effects of this misguided tactic are clearly predicted in the Bible. Most adherents to this philosophy are unaware that they could be setting the stage for the appearance of the Beast, or the ultimate Antichrist. Even Christians are much too often in the dark about the implications of this development. They don't realize that these deadly predators could become one of the Beast's important tools to accomplish his agenda for the human race, but that is exactly what these animals could do. Read on as I attempt to make this assertion clear to the reader.

NOTES

1 J. Park, "Human Languages: Resources from Linguistics and Beyond," *C & RL News*, Vol. 66, No. 3, March 2005.

2 *Science Daily*, February 21, 2008, Massachusetts Institute of Technology (quoting Dr. Robert Berwick, MIT Department of Brain and Cognitive Sciences).

3 Stefan Hiendleder, et al, "Molecular Analyses of Wild and Domestic Sheep Questions Current Nomenclature and Provides Evidence of Domestication from Two Different Subspecies," *Proceedings: Biological Sciences*, Vol. 269, No. 1494, May 7, 2002, 893-904.

4 Associated Press, www.myyellowstonewolves.typepad.com/myw/2008/04/index.html, April 28, 2008 [accessed May 19, 2009].

FIVE

Animals and
The Law of Moses

It's Against the Law *Not* to Use Animals

"THE Law of Moses" and "The Mosaic Law" are two ways of saying the same thing, and both are a bit of a misnomer. However, this terminology has been deeply ingrained over the centuries, so either is commonly used in interchangeable fashion. In fact, this Law was not given by any human agency, Moses or otherwise, but was given directly to Moses by God (Exodus 20-40; most of Leviticus; and significant parts of Numbers and Deuteronomy). God actually wrote the centerpiece of the Law with His finger on two tablets of stone (the Ten Commandments, Deuteronomy 9:10), and these Moses was commissioned to deliver to the Israelite nation, a stubborn lot if ever there was one. Their outlook and values seem so very similar to our own country today that it is scary to contemplate. After one false start caused by the sin of the people, Moses managed to get down the mountain with a second set of tablets intact.

Much of the Mosaic Law was already being practiced by believing Children of Israel, such as prohibitions against murder and homosexual activity. Among the Israelites, as with practically any society, there was a contingent that sought God to know His will and apply it to all areas of life, but a significantly larger group wanted God out of their lives completely—does this sound familiar? That this is so in the case of Israel during the time of Moses is easily demonstrated by the general

61

intransigence of the Israelites to the important call God had given them to be His representatives, His chosen people, in the world. They were to do this by following perfectly the Law they had been given, and by their faith and obedience showing the very presence of God to the world. This proved to be an impossible task, no doubt not a surprise to God, since even Moses himself found keeping the Law perfectly to be beyond his capabilities. Both the Apostle Paul and the author of Hebrews, in the New Testament, make it abundantly clear that the Law was never intended to make people behave perfectly. It served simply as a standard and a constant reminder of the need for blood atonement to cover sins until the perfect sacrifice arrived at the proper time.

Of course, like life in general, the Mosaic Law wasn't just about animals, though the sacrificial aspects of the law almost always involved animals, either "clean" animals, as defined by the Law, or "clean" birds, usually a pigeon or dove. The Law prescribed sacrifice of certain animals for certain offenses, and the offering on the altar—which was at the time yet to be built in a permanent place—of all or part of the carcass. Different kinds of offerings are described in detail, mainly in the Book of Leviticus and in Numbers 28-29, with further instructions in Deuteronomy 12. The manner of killing the animal is not usually expressed, except that it had to be done so the blood could be drained away. Often the exact way the carcass was to be divided and offered on the altar is described.

Two pervasive items concerning animal usage emerge from a reading of these portions of the Law: First, the blood was sprinkled in various manners, but never left in the dead animal, never consumed by the people, and never offered up as a burnt offering. The life of the flesh is in the blood, and eating it showed disrespect for the Creator of life; it was to be sprinkled on the horns of the altar and the rest poured out at the base of the altar. Second, human consumption of the more palatable parts (red muscle drained of blood but no internal organs) was perfectly acceptable in certain cases. There is no question that, under the Mosaic Law, God thoroughly sanctioned eating the flesh of clean animals. It is highly interesting that the parts least healthful for human consumption (the internal organs, the blood, and the fat) were not to be eaten. How would Moses, with only the highly-flawed science of ancient Egypt as background, ever have known about cholesterol, apart from supernatural insight? This is simply more evidence that the Bible is accurate.

Animal sacrifice was a cornerstone of the Law, *temporarily* covering man's transgressions against a perfectly holy God. The Ten Commandments were of utmost importance and, at first glance, this well-known set of rules seems to have nothing at all to do with animal sacrifice. However, in every instance, disobeying God by failing to observe one of these commandments (or any other part of the Law) had only one specific remedy: the sacrifice of an animal. This sacrifice, as already noted, served to temporarily cover a transgression against God and His perfect Law. Each year, on the Day of Atonement, a corporate sacrifice was performed to cover the sins of the people committed during the previous year, while individual sins also required smaller sacrifices throughout the year. Never does the Law indicate sin is permanently wiped away by these sacrifices; it only indicates that by a person's obedience to what they knew, the transgression was temporarily covered until the perfect sacrifice—Jesus Christ, the faultless "lamb" of God—appeared.

Thou Shall Not Kill?

While we are on the subject of the Ten Commandments, let's address the important order, "Thou shall not kill." Animal rights proponents often cite this as justification for their position advocating an absolute moratorium on animal deaths at the hands of human beings. By holding this erroneous viewpoint, it is clear they are not doing their homework. The word for kill in the Hebrew is accurately translated "murder."

There is a general word for "kill," and it is not used in the commandment. *Murder* is committed only if a human being unlawfully kills another human being, whether or not there was malicious intent.[1] Clarification is provided in Genesis 1:27, where it states "God created man in His own image." In Genesis 9:6 it states "Whoever sheds man's blood, By man his blood shall be shed, For in the image of God He made man." As noted previously, this is reiterated in several places in the Mosaic Law, perhaps most clearly in Leviticus 24:21. Murder is murder not because a kill takes place, as animal rights advocates insist; murder is committed

NOTES ON CLEAN AND UNCLEAN ANIMALS
(Leviticus 11 and Deuteronomy 14)

CLEAN	UNCLEAN	NOTES
(1) Ox (cattle) Sheep Goat	(6) Camel Rabbit Coney (likely the rock badger, marmot, or woodchuck)	(1) Clean mammals (domestic and wild) have long digestive tracts and ruminate, or regurgitate and re-chew their food; they also have split hooves (plus long legs—see 11).
(2) Deer Gazelle Roe deer Wild goat Ibex Antelope Mountain sheep	(7) Pig (8) Eagle Vultures Kites Ravens Owls	(2-5) Some form of hunting would be necessary to kill and eat any of these listed clean animals (see Leviticus 17:13-14). Each is almost always taken from the wild. (2) Biblical accuracy: The ibex and wild goat are listed separately; interestingly, they have been found scientifically to be separate species. The same is true of deer and roe deer.
(3) Any bird not listed as unclean	Ostrich Pelican Gull Hawks Falcons Osprey Cormorant Stork Heron Hoopoe	(3) Even songbirds are edible! (see Matthew 10:29-30). (4) This eliminates most aquatic scavengers. (5) All these are flying insects that walk on four front legs and have jointed back legs for jumping.
(4) Water creatures with fins and scales	(9) Bat (10) All flying and swarming insects	(6) Some unclean animals appear to chew the cud; however, they don't have split hooves. The horse and donkey are not listed anywhere, along with many other mammals, probably because it is clear they have neither required characteristic (e.g., elephant, hippopotamus). The same is true of mammalian predators.
(5) Locust Katydid Cricket Grasshopper	(11) Weasel Rat All lizards Skink Chameleon	(7) Pigs have split hooves but are omnivorous and are scavengers. They have short digestive tracts (like man) and tend to carry diseases that could affect man. (8) Predatory birds or carrion-eaters. (9) Listed last among flying creatures to set it apart; the Bible does not list the bat as a bird. (10) All insects were unclean except the four listed as clean. (11) These animals moved "along the ground," indicating a possible connection between cleanliness and length of the legs. Snakes are not listed, but under this assumption, as well as Biblical history, these would be the ultimate in uncleanness.

only when men insult God Himself by killing one of His image-bearers. This is the basis of the command, which is more accurately rendered "Thou shall not murder another human being." The *Meat is Murder* bumper sticker I observe from time to time (particularly ironic when accompanied by a pro-choice sticker) reveals the gullibility and ignorance of the driver of that car.

The sacrifices outlined in the Old Testament also provided for another specific need: Food for the priests and their families. For certain sacrifices, God mandated that a predetermined portion be consumed as food by those serving as priests, to be shared by their dependents. The rest of the edible portion was also usually to be eaten, either by the person offering the sacrifice (and their family), or by the people of Israel in general, especially during appointed feasts. Some special sacrifices, such as certain sin offerings, were not to be eaten, but were to be offered on the altar and then completely burned up outside the camp.

There are great numbers of sacrifices offered to God throughout the Old Testament after the time of Moses. For example, King Solomon's dedication of the original temple in Jerusalem was an occasion of sacrifice of "so many sheep and oxen that they could not be counted or numbered" (2 Chronicles 5:6) and still another sacrifice shortly thereafter of "22,000 oxen and 120,000 sheep" (2 Chronicles 7:5). God was highly pleased with these sacrifices, as evidenced by the fact that He appeared immediately afterward and spoke to Solomon personally (2 Chronicles 7:12-22). No one can justify opposition to animal utilization and taking the lives of animals based on the Bible!

A few centuries later, two of the greatest prophets in the Bible are linked in 1 Kings 19:21, when the older man began the process of passing his office on to the younger. The younger man, Elisha, was heir to the prophet Elijah, one of only two men in the Bible who did not die, but were taken up by God alive (2 Kings 2:11-12); the other was the pre-flood prophet, Enoch (Genesis 5:18-24; Hebrews 11:5). Elisha "took a pair of oxen and sacrificed them and boiled their flesh with the implements of the oxen, and gave it to the people and they ate. Then he arose and followed Elijah and ministered to him." This act was in no way condemned by Elijah or by God.

Lest the reader infer that only animals sacrificed in the temple according to the Law could be eaten, consider the following. Deuteronomy 12:15-27 gives instruction for the Israelites just before they entered the Promised Land. Here the long years of wilderness wandering were about to come to an end, and God realized that many of His people would live too far from the central worship location to bring any animal to be killed for food or clothing to that location. To require this would have made many of the people unable to utilize meat and skins unless they journeyed to Jerusalem to sacrifice the animal. A distinction is clearly made between "holy" sacrifices in the temple, and "secular" sacrifices for food that would necessarily be performed at home. Killing domestic animals in a location far from Jerusalem is compared to killing and eating animals taken by hunting: Drain the blood and then the people were free to eat the animal and otherwise utilize its parts. With both "holy" sacrifices performed at the temple and "secular" sacrifices made at home or on the hunting grounds, the blood was to be drained from the animal and not eaten, but the flesh was to be consumed by the people.

Consider also that clean fish (those with scales and fins) seem to be excluded from the sacrificial system, yet fishermen and the consumption of fish are highly prominent in the Bible. At least seven of Jesus' twelve disciples were fishermen, in fact. There can be no doubt that the Law sanctions consumption of fish, and, as with most birds, there was little or no legal or ritual requirement to such consumption.

It appears in several places that there will be both fishing and fishermen in Christ's future Kingdom on earth. For example, Ezekiel 47 describes the Dead Sea as becoming fresh water at that time and holding huge swarms of fish. It goes on to describe how fishermen will spread their nets along the shoreline of a body of water currently devoid of practically all living creatures. Fishing nets mean, without any question, the catching of fish for food. This is yet additional proof that animal consumption will continue to be sanctioned during the Millennial reign of Christ. The modern nation of Israel has actually considered tunneling across the Judean Mountains to send water to the shrinking Dead Sea for purposes of generating unlimited hydroelectric power,[2] a massive engineering project that would actually make the Dead Sea into inhabitable waters for sea life, should it ever be accomplished. Making the Dead Sea into truly fresh water would require a supernatural event, such as described in Ezekiel 47, but it appears clear to me that this actually could happen one day (see also Revelation 22:1).

That fish are left out of the sacrificial system is probably more a matter of practicality than anything else. Getting live fish from the Sea of Galilee or the Great Sea (the Mediterranean) would have presented an insurmountable challenge in those days of slow travel and water containers of limited size and mobility. All animal sacrifices had to be "living sacrifices," meaning they were killed only at the time they were offered.

Someone may say, "All right, commercial fishing, meat eating, and animal sacrifice are all there, but doesn't all this indicate that killing animals by hunting is wrong?" On the contrary, Isaac sent his son Esau into the field to hunt and kill some wild game for him in Genesis 27. Additionally, the Law itself covers hunting quite positively; the procedure for dealing with a bird or animal killed while hunting is given in Leviticus 17:13. It refers to clean animals, as described extensively elsewhere in the Law where it stresses, remarkably, those animals most healthful to eat and least likely to carry diseases. The bottom line is that the hunter must immediately drain the creature's blood onto the ground (and cover it with soil) so its cooking and eating will be according to the Law. While freedom in Christ means that we are no longer bound by this procedure, it is still good advice. I always immediately field dress any game I kill while hunting, removing most of the blood along with the heart, lungs, and entrails, usually within minutes of my shot, which dramatically improves the flavor and tenderness of the meat.

The Law of Moses also contains very clearly in several places the concept of sustainable utilization of animal resources, including wild animals. For example, in Deuteronomy 22:6-7 we are told that ancient Israelites were free to take from a bird nest either eggs or young birds, but they were forbidden to take the mother bird at the same time. She represented the ability, like domestic laying hens, to produce another nest with more eggs and young right away. In the wild, it is actually very common for a nesting bird to lose its eggs or young,[3] at which point, in most cases, another nest is quickly created, resulting in no net loss to the species.

That God sanctions clean animals of all kinds for food according to the Law cannot be denied. That He expanded this to include *all* animal flesh as appropriate for consumption in the New Testament is a concept we will explore later in a number of important contexts and in several prominent passages.

NOTES

1 Calvin Lashway, www.biblestudy.org/question/what-does-thou-shalt-not-kill-mean.html, [accessed Feb. 2009—search under "The Ten Commandments"].

2 www.meddead.org/MedDead_Peace_Initiative.html, [accessed Feb. 2009; same information found on numerous additional websites].

3 S. Bensch and Hasselquis, "Higher Rate of Nest Loss among Primary than Secondary Females," *Behavioral Ecology and Sociobiology*, Vol. 35, No. 5, Nov. 1994, 309-317.

SIX

GOD'S JUDGMENT THROUGH ANIMALS

I N this short section I will cover mainly the Old Testament instances where God used animals to bring down His wrath on mankind. There are a number of these, and some of them look forward to a time when the Almighty's wrath will be released on the unbelieving world in a far more broad-reaching and devastating fashion. As much as possible, I will adhere to isolated incidents confined to the Old Testament, and I will save the horrifying role predicted for animals during the future tribulation for Chapter Twelve.

Perhaps the earliest and most obvious uses of animals for judgment occurred in the Book of Exodus (chapters 5-14). Here several species were used to torment the Egyptians, with the objective of convincing them to release their Israelite slaves, who had served them for more than four hundred years. Frogs, gnats, flies, death of livestock, death of aquatic creatures, and a plague of locusts eating all the crops and green plants—all were used full force against the Egyptians and their pharaoh. More than half of the ten devastations God perpetrated against the Egyptians involved animals of some kind, and all were severe to the utmost. None of the first nine plagues, however, was effective in convincing the Egyptian leader to release the Israelites. Only the last plague, the death of every first-born creature in Egypt, of both man and beast, was finally able to accomplish this. Even after this last disaster and their release, the pharaoh changed his mind and tried to re-enslave Israel by sending his army in pursuit. He and his entire force of soldiers, chariots, and horses perished in the Red Sea while engaged in this futile effort (Exodus 14).

When the Law of Moses was given at Sinai, it actually included the use of predators as a means of enforcing obedience. In Leviticus 26:6, God promises to "eliminate harmful beasts from the land" if the Israelites would follow His Law carefully. In a following passage, God gives the opposite for disobedience, promising to loose wild "beasts of the field, which shall bereave you of your children and destroy your cattle and reduce your number so that your roads lie deserted" (Leviticus 26:22). This establishes a historical precedent for the increase in animal attacks we are seeing in our world today. This gruesome vengeance obviously came upon the Israelites in ancient times, and will again be meted out at some point in the future all over the world. What we are seeing today in the increased numbers of attacks on humans by wild beasts[1] is simply another instance foreshadowing a major change to come. This is an awful scenario we will cover more thoroughly in Chapter Twelve.

While the Children of Israel were still wandering in the desert for forty years because of their rebellion against God, they again revolted in Numbers 21:5. I have already mentioned that the nomadic Israelites were a regrettably difficult and complaining people, so very much like those of us who live in modern times. In this case, God sent among them "fiery serpents" (Numbers 21:6), which bit and killed many people because of their murmuring against Moses. These would have been venomous snakes with quite a lethal bite. The people pleaded with Moses to save them from these deadly reptiles (Numbers 21:7), so he prayed to God and received instructions on how his people could avoid death from such a bite (Numbers 21:8-9). He was instructed to set up a bronze serpent so that when a person was bitten, all they had to do was look at the standard in order to live. In John 3:14-15, Jesus Christ refers to this incident as being metaphorical of His sacrifice on the cross for the sins of mankind, and the need to believe in order to be saved. In both cases, one must believe in order to look to the means of salvation and live, physically in the first case and spiritually in the second.

In Ezekiel 5:17 and 14:15, a plague of wild beasts is pronounced against sinful man, with particular focus on Israel. When combined with accompanying afflictions in Ezekiel 14, the scenario is highly reminiscent of certain judgments found in the book of Revelation. We will go into this in more detail later, because it appears that the animal rights movement will set the stage for fulfillment of some of these predicted disasters.

North of Jerusalem is a town named Bethel. The name means "House of God," and it is where the patriarch Jacob, later named Israel, dreamed of a golden stairway leading to Heaven and heard God speak to him (Genesis 28:11-19). In one prominent instance found in 2 Kings 2:23-24, a crowd of youths from this town jeered and taunted the prophet Elisha as he walked along the road. Elisha cursed them in the name of the Lord, and immediately two bears emerged from the woods and tore up 42 of their number. Whether anyone was killed or not isn't stated. Native to the area are Mideastern brown bears (*Ursus arctos syriacus*), the same species as our North American grizzly bear,[2] and they are easily capable of maiming and killing with little effort. Suffice it to say it isn't wise to make fun of a true prophet of God, as those youths found out to their sorrow.

Another well-known incident of "animal judgment" involves the prophet Daniel. According to the book of Daniel, he had become, because of his godliness and wisdom, a very high official of King Darius, whose Medo-Persian empire succeeded Babylon in dominating the known world. Other contemporary officials, moved by jealousy, continually sought to find fault with Daniel, but no matter how hard they tried, they were unable to do so. Knowing full well that Daniel prayed to God three times a day, they devised a plot to use this faithfulness against him. They proposed to unsuspecting King Darius that he issue an irreversible edict that no one in his kingdom could pray to any god or man except him for a period of time. The penalty for violation was also decreed, and it was severe. Any person found praying to anyone besides the king was to be cast into a cavern filled with fierce, hungry lions (Daniel 6:7-8). Why King Darius would consent to give such an order is not apparent, though it was possibly presented to him when he was preoccupied with other pressing business. It is known that he held

Daniel in highest esteem, and it seems unlikely that King Darius would be oblivious to his prayer habits. Whatever the case, the jealous officials had their way and the king issued and sealed the edict so that it couldn't be altered. I am reminded of how present-day bureaucrats usually seem to get their way, even when their rulings and decrees are clearly at odds with the thinking and philosophy of their superiors.

It was evidently only a short time before these officials caught Daniel doing what their hatched-up edict specifically forbade—praying to the one true God (it would have worked for their purposes had he prayed to some pagan god or to a mere man other than the king, for that matter). Too late the king realized he had been tricked into signing such an order, and he did everything possible to avoid having to place Daniel in the den of lions. Such a written, signed, and sealed declaration could not be changed, according to the prevailing law, even by the king who issued it, so Darius eventually was forced to do what he didn't want to do. He ordered Daniel placed in with the lions and committed him to the care of the God he knew Daniel served (Daniel 6:16).

The king then spent a night without food or sleep, and early the next morning he ran to the lion's den to see what had happened. Daniel was unharmed because God had sent an angel to close the lions' mouths (Daniel 6:22). After checking Daniel over and finding him without so much as a scratch, the king's anger immediately turned toward those officials who had arranged such a trap, and he had them, along with their wives and children, thrown in with the lions. Not surprisingly, no angel was there to keep the lions at bay for these murderous officials, and the Bible states that the lions rushed upon them even before they reached the floor of the den and "crushed all their bones" (Daniel 6:24).

Ghastly Premonitions

On the very day I originally wrote this section, there were three awful animal attacks, one a deadly attack by a shark in North Carolina[3] and two near-fatal attacks by alligators in Florida[4] and Lousiana.[5] As I conducted a review some months later, two confined tigers attacked two people in Missouri, and did horrible damage to them.[6] Cougar attacks in California, where cougar hunting has been banned since 1972, are so common that several web sites keep track of the increasing trend.[7]

Such events are becoming so common they are hardly newsworthy anymore, even when scores of people are left dead. (For example, did you hear about this referenced loss of life?[8] These attacks were by a variety of animals, with elephants and crocodiles at the top of the killer list.) Remember, these creatures still are under the essential God-imposed terror of man established immediately after the flood of Noah (Genesis 9:2), yet they attack people with increasing frequency. I do not believe any given instance can be traced solely to the sins of the individual who has suffered an animal attack; however, I do believe that the deterioration of our whole value system as a people has allowed a general lowering of God's protective barrier between man and animals. Innocents may suffer as a consequence, but the whole human race is at fault. Eventually, all God's protection will be removed and the results will be devastating.

These unfortunate examples are only warnings of terrible times to come. God's ultimate use of animals to execute vengeance is personified by the true man of sin, or Antichrist, about whom I will have much more to say later. This individual actually will be fully human, but will have so many animalistic characteristics that he is frequently referred to in the Bible as "the Beast." Chapter Twelve has much more to say about this coming ruler.

The worst is yet ahead, in my opinion. We will cover in much detail the horrendous role animals could play, to the delight of the Beast, during that brief but what I believe are terrible times to come.

NOTES

1 www.foxnews.com/story/0,2933,280492,00.html, "Surge in Wild Animal Attacks on Suburban Children," Monday June 11, 2007 [accessed Feb. 2009].

2 Safari Club International's *Record Book of Trophy Animals*, Ed. Ten, 252.

3 J. Allegood, "Second Shark Bite on N.C. Coast," *The News & Observer*, Raleigh-Durham, NC, July 18, 2007.

4 "Florida Teen Loses Arm in Alligator Attack," *The Associated Press*, June 24, 2008.

5 "Doctors Unable to Save Boy's Arm after Gator Attack," *The New Orleans Times-Picayune*, July 31, 2008.

6 B. Taylor, "Teen Badly Injured in Second Missouri Tiger Attack in Two Days," *The Associated Press*, Aug. 4, 2008.

7 tchester.org/sgm/lists/lion_attacks_ca.html; www.topangaonline.com/nature/lionatk.html; www.dfg.ca.gov/news/issues/lion/attacks.html.

8 Vivi Black, "Wild Animals Kill 133 in Mozambique," *Citizen Journalism Report*, March 18, 2008.

SEVEN

BIBLICAL STEWARDSHIP
OF ANIMALS

Animal Enemy: Vegetables

IT is an interesting statistic that the animals consumed most often by man for food are also the most numerous animals on earth. There are more than one billion domestic sheep in the world (as opposed to 15 million wild white-tailed deer, for example). Those animals not used for food, and particularly those singled out for special protection, are the rarest. Most of the time rarity of an animal comes about because it is deprived by man of critical habitat, and much of the time that habitat is used for growing what vegetarians prefer—fruits, vegetables, nuts, and grain.

Man's mandate to make the fields yield their fruit is as valid today as in the beginning when Adam was actually created in part to be a cultivator of the ground (Genesis 2:5). However, it is a fact that loss of habitat is probably the major reason for declines in wildlife populations, though this usually results from simple mismanagement of the available land. In Europe, one seldom sees prime agricultural land being converted to subdivisions, while in the USA this is commonplace. The same could be said of prime wildlife habitat on the two sides of the Atlantic. Still, pragmatic people here recognize the need to set aside sufficient habitat for wild creatures, a concept in which outdoorsmen have been leaders for generations. In America, with proper planning and execution, there is plenty of room for agriculture, reasonable development of land for human usage, and land for wildlife habitat.

Vegetarians, at least those with an animal rights mentality, may not like the fact that there are so many animals raised for human food. They may also blame others for any declines in wildlife populations, since they don't "consumptively" use wildlife or even domestic stock. But they can't wiggle out of a share of responsibility, since growing the plants they prefer also occupies vast tracts of land made unsuitable in many cases for either wildlife or domestic-stock purposes.

In California, I have first-hand knowledge of one wild species that is a victim of the human appetite for vegetables. The tule elk was almost exterminated for its meat during the California gold rush of the mid-1800s, and fewer than ten individual animals survived.[1] Today these elk have recovered to about four thousand in number, making them still one of the rarest native wild ungulates (hoofed animals) of the Americas. However, the reason they have not returned to their historical levels, like other subspecies of North American elk, is purely because their ancient habitat is now California's vegetable, fruit, nut, and wine heartland. While major steps have been taken to set aside significant public lands for the elk, and to encourage private landowners to make room for them, there will probably never be more than a few thousand of these creatures in California because of sprawling but essential agricultural cropland. Still, efforts to accommodate the elk continue even today, encouraged by true conservationists such as sportsmen.[2]

God's blessing unquestionably rests upon the usage of animals for food, clothing, and other products. During the time before Christ, He also blessed the sacrifice of animals as a temporary covering for and reminder of man's sin, with the real price being paid by Christ's blood at the proper time. Many interpret the book of Ezekiel as indicating that animal sacrifices will be offered once more as a memorial of Christ's sacrifice during His reign on the earth, or else by Jews who feel a sense of piety in a hoped for restored temple (and who are unaware of the once-for-all sacrifice of Christ) (Hebrews 7:27, cf. Ezekiel 43:10-11).

Biblical Animal Welfare

Using animals even for legitimate purposes, however, does not give anyone the right to abuse them. Deuteronomy is a book whose title literally means "second giving" of the Mosaic Law. It is directed at the surviving generation of Israelites that would actually enter and conquer the Promised Land, after their parents died in the wilderness, being prohibited because of rebellion from entering. It states that one "shall not muzzle the ox while he is threshing" (Deuteronomy 25:4). This recognizes the duty of man to care for his animals and give working creatures a just reward for labor performed. In the New Testament, this concept is expanded to have a broader application to man in his work, establishing the principle that the working man should share in the fruits of his labor (1 Corinthians 9:9-10). The passage clearly asks whether God is concerned about oxen at all! From many other passages, He is obviously interested in the *welfare* of oxen, but this concern quite clearly pales in comparison to that held for His image-bearer.

God was assuredly interested in human exercise of good animal stewardship when He dictated the Law to Moses. He gives numerous rules to govern various situations involving livestock, largely concentrated in Exodus 21-22. There are references in the Old Testament about providing well for one's livestock, such as the command in Exodus 23:12 to allow working animals to rest on the Sabbath, just as man was to rest.

The principle of caring well for animals is carried over into the New Testament. Jesus was criticized by the Jewish leaders of the day for healing sick people on the Sabbath, and he responded that they also worked on the Sabbath. Two examples he used were pulling their sheep out of a pit if one got into such trouble on a Sabbath (Matthew 12:11); and taking their means of transportation (a donkey or ox) to water on the Sabbath (Luke 13:15).

I sometimes find myself in some degree of sympathy with animal rights advocates, no matter how erroneous their overall philosophy may be, when they point out cases of outright abuse of animals in such ways as dog fighting, crowded and unsanitary living conditions for penned animals, savage beatings of animals, neglect in providing adequate food and shelter, and all such instances of outright inhumane treatment. This is not to say that animal rights fanatics are the only ones to point out such exploitation, since any ethical person would report these activities to authorities. However, there is a major gulf between animal *rights* and animal *welfare*. Most people of a normally sensitive mindset are enthusiastic advocates of animal welfare, and believe in prosecution of people who engage in animal cruelty, as defined by most current laws in our country. Mankind has used animals ethically and compassionately for thousands of years by making certain they are protected, fed, watered, and given shelter as necessary. Caring for animals under your personal stewardship is a God-ordained duty that we should take quite seriously. To do otherwise is unquestionably sinful, slothful, and to be condemned. Absolutely nothing in the realm of animal welfare, however, conflicts with the utilization of animals in an ethical, traditional fashion.

I believe it is the rare farmer who intentionally mistreats his animals, because of the very practical fact that neglect and abuse lead to reduced productivity and a lower-quality product. The Bible is full of references, both direct and by inference, of people treating animals well, even though such creatures were used for food, clothing, shelter, transportation, sacrifice, and dairy products, among other things. There is a way to keep animals in a manner that cares intently for their well-being yet allows for their sustainable utilization as prudent and necessary.

Jacob, in Genesis 30, cared well for his herds of animals and began a selective breeding program that made him rich (unfortunately at the expense of his father-in-law). He could not have had such success had he abused the animals in his flocks. Moses was a herdsman for forty years in the land of Midian (Exodus 2-3), where he married his wife and had children. He clearly gave great attention to his father-in-law's flocks and herds, and one can assume that they prospered, though there is no specific mention of this.

Sheep and People

Whenever I am in a foreign land, I try to notice the herding practices there. I have seen herding in perhaps forty countries, and in most places flocks and herds are accompanied by a human caretaker. For some reason I always think of the shepherd boy David when I am privileged to see such an activity. David, the shepherd of the sheep, later became king of Israel, where he led the people of ancient Israel like a shepherd. Sheep particularly need constant care, and so do people. The shepherd and the sheep are a picture of God's care for people, and sheep are repeatedly used to refer figuratively to God's people.

This concept is found throughout the Bible, but has its greatest expression in the life of Jesus Christ. His status as a coming shepherd is found often in the Old Testament, where this exact function was predicted by several prophets. Perhaps the most famous Psalm is the 23rd, which starts out with the words, "The Lord is my shepherd...." In Isaiah 40:10-11, a Messianic passage where the prophet states "like a shepherd He will tend His flock." Another important passage is in Jeremiah 3:15, where God promises that He will give Israel "shepherds after My own heart, who will feed you on knowledge and understanding." Many believe these will be godly, human leaders who serve in Christ's Kingdom, since it is plural.

Later in that same book (Jeremiah 23:1-4), God condemns as worthless "shepherds who are destroying and scattering the sheep of My pasture." He promises that He will become their shepherd and set godly leaders over them. Rejection of God as the Good Shepherd occurs in Zechariah 11 and, as a consequence, God announces His intention to place worthless shepherds over Israel, shepherds who would not care for the good of the nation, but instead would plunder it. This reminds me of present-day politicians, too many of whom serve only themselves. The prophet Micah, in verses 5:2, 4, promises that out of the tribe of Judah would come a "ruler in Israel" who will "shepherd His flock in the strength of the LORD." This prophecy is fulfilled seven hundred years later in the person of Jesus Christ.

In the New Testament, Jesus is repeatedly called both a shepherd, in recognition of His lordship over all creation, as well as a lamb, referring to His perfect sacrifice, the only one adequate to pay for the sins of mankind. The first New Testament reference to Him being a shepherd is in Matthew 2:6, which repeats the prophecy of Micah 5:2, and in practically every book down through Revelation Jesus either refers to Himself as a shepherd or is referred to by another inspired writer as a shepherd. In Revelation 7:17 He is called both a lamb and a shepherd. Examples of His shepherd status are found in John 10:11, where Jesus states "I am the good shepherd; the good shepherd lays down His life for the sheep." In 1 Peter 2:25, Jesus is referred to as "the Shepherd and Guardian of your souls."

In Hebrews 13:20, He is called "the great Shepherd of the sheep." Other instances such as these are pervasive in both the Old and New Testaments.

Use Animals (But With Care)

In fact, almost every book of the Bible has some reference to sheep and shepherds, and/or to other animals, with the number of individual passages well into the hundreds, far too numerous to catalog in this work. By far the majority of these references are in the context of utilization of these animals for man's benefit. Good shepherding and caring for other domestic stock was a cornerstone of that herding culture, just as the good farmer (or shepherd still, in most countries) must care for his livestock in order to see prosperity. Furthermore, bad shepherding leads to poverty and disaster. Being good to your animals and caring for them well is vital to using them in sustainable fashion, and it has always been that way. No abused animal will live up to its potential and produce the kind of benefit its owner desires.

The obvious conclusion is that shepherds, shepherding, and utilization of flocks as sacrifices, food, and clothing are all eminently acceptable to God.

By the same token, poor treatment of animals is condemned in several places in the Bible. In Proverbs 27:23-27, for example, it states in summary that a person should know well the condition of his herds by paying adequate attention to them. By this one is assured of plentiful clothing (sheep skins), trading goods (sheep and goats), as well as meat and milk for one's household. Proverbs 12:10 states that, "A righteous man has regard for the life of his beast, But the compassion of the wicked is cruel."

There is not a single reference in the Bible that criticizes competent animal husbandry or the raising of animals for the benefit of human beings. On the contrary, utilization of animals is the norm in both the Old and New Testaments. Scriptural references to eating meat, especially of sheep, goats, and cattle, are far too extensive to list exhaustively. There are hundreds of them, and not a single one is critical of the practice. As I made clear earlier, eating meat was not a matter of convenience in those days; it was absolutely essential to good health, just as it is today for most of mankind. Jesus made it clear to his disciples that "'whatever goes into the man from outside cannot defile him; because it does not go into his heart, but into his stomach, and is eliminated…' (Thus He declared all foods clean*)" (Mark 7:18-19). That would include any animal a person has the need or desire to eat. The apostle Peter, in 2 Peter 2:12, refers to "unreasoning animals, born as creatures of instinct to be captured and killed."

That animals are sentient beings is undeniable, because they have senses of smell, hearing, vision, etc., and they certainly react to stimuli. The animal rights movement is always criticizing our utilization of animals because they are sentient. However, this only means they possess nerve connections which reveal to them their environment, so even plants could be called "sentient" by loosening this definition only slightly. However many senses animals may possess, they are nonetheless incapable of calculated thinking or reasoning on the same level as and equal to man. Since Peter claims that animals are "unreasoning," one can dismiss or ignore the rampant anthropomorphism in everything from Disney movies to kids' television programs, which is sometimes undisguised animal rights propaganda. There is more to this passage in 2 Peter that needs to be detailed, and this I will do in Chapter Nine.

The unreasoning nature of animals is by no means a New Testament concept, either. For example, King David was a shepherd as a youth who vigorously defended his flocks against all threats (e.g., 1 Samuel 17:34-36). However, he recognized the limitations of animals and wrote in Psalm 32:9, "Do not be as the horse or as the mule which have no understanding, Whose trappings include bit and bridle to hold them in check, Otherwise they will not come near to you." No doubt David had considerable experience with all kinds of animals and he knew that they are sentient only in possessing the same five basic senses as human beings. However, he was also clear in indicating that they are incapable of calculated thought processes at the same level as humans.

In the book of Acts (10:10-13), this same apostle Peter, who spent all the years of Jesus' earthly ministry in His personal presence, was presented a remarkable vision. A great sheet descended out of the sky in

---

* This may be a marginal note appended to the text, as it appears in the NASB and mainstreamed via the Majority Text. The Textus Receptus (King James) does not contain the parenthetical text at all. –Ed.

this vision, and it was filled with all kinds of animals that practicing Jews considered "unclean" and thus inedible. Peter was directed by the voice of God to "Get up, Peter, kill and eat!" This is a direct command, and one which cannot be obeyed if one is a vegetarian or insists on following the Old Testament Law. Peter protests not the killing but the *kinds* of "unclean" animals God presents as newly edible. He is nonetheless told by that same voice that "What God has cleansed, no longer consider unholy." God was apparently re-emphasizing what Jesus had taught his disciples in Mark 7:18-19, where He declared man could not be defiled by what he consumes. This demonstration to Peter happened three times to stress that all living creatures were now once more (as they had been before the giving of the Law) available to all people, including Jews, as food. It also served to say emphatically that entering a Gentile (non-Jewish) household was now permissible, something that had previously made a Jew ceremonially "unclean."

Peter repeats this story to the other apostles in Acts 11, which doubly emphasizes that Christians possess great latitude in selecting their desired food down to this very day. Had these incidents and directives not occurred, every Christian would be required to refrain from pork, shrimp, oysters, lobster, catfish, scallops, and many other kinds of delicious meat common today. This release from the constraints of the Law (or more accurately Jesus' fulfillment of the Law) made it much easier to reach out to non-Jews in the name of Christ. Other provisions of the Law, such as circumcision, were also eliminated, apparently as God's plan to facilitate spread of the good news of His Son's death to pay our penalty for sin, His resurrection in power, and His offer of eternal life to all who respond by faith to believe. External factors such as prohibited foods and male circumcision were no longer necessary to set a person apart as a follower of God and receive His plan for their life. The indispensable internal factor of the indwelling Holy Spirit was now the essential dynamic that set apart the people of God, whatever their race or nationality.

From all this Biblical information it is easy to understand that God created animals for the benefit and enjoyment of mankind, unless one is willfully blind. We are expected to herd them, hunt them, kill them, ride them, and utilize them, but to do so in a humane and efficient manner. There is to be nothing slothful or unholy about our utilization of animals. Knowing something of the nature of God, I believe that we are to do all these things so that it creates as little suffering as possible. Slitting the throat of an animal is akin to cutting off its head or putting a gunshot to the head. In slitting the carotid arteries, there is sudden loss of blood flow to the brain. This causes immediate unconsciousness, so there is probably not even a faint perception of pain. A well-placed bullet does essentially the same thing, in addition to causing massive terminal contusion of the brain. When I am hunting deer for meat, which I do regularly during deer season, I always make a head shot to minimize suffering. This also facilitates retrieval of the animal, as a shot to the head causes the animal to drop in its tracks. I often wait until a deer is where I want it to fall before shooting, and then I immediately go to the animal, thank God for it, and proceed with field dressing it to remove internal organs and blood right away. My meat is thus totally untainted and wholesome.

I only wish I could have an animal rights activist sit down to one of my wife's meals of cubed venison rolled in wheat flour and fried in olive oil, accompanied by garden-fresh vegetables baked, or occasionally fried, in this same fashion. It is beyond any doubt one of the healthiest diets a person can eat. I only hope the whole world doesn't take to it, because the estimated fifteen million white-tailed deer in the USA wouldn't be nearly enough to feed everyone. I do hope this book will contribute to the non-hunting population accepting hunting and other legitimate animal utilization as what it is: Normal, Bible-based, God-ordained, Christ-sanctified, and necessary for optimum health and well-being.

For the truly fortunate, God-blessed individual like me, it's the only way to go.

NOTES

1 "Tule Elk: The Return of a Species," National Park Service Resource Paper, 1998, www.nps.gov.

2 M. Fay, "Finding Space for Tule Elk," Patagonia Enviro Essay, www.patagonia.com, Jan. 2008.

EIGHT

THE RELATIONSHIP OF
JESUS TO ANIMALS

Jesus Can Kill?

SOME appear to have a view of Jesus Christ that grows out of fairyland, likening Him to the Hindu sage Mahatma Gandhi, a person who wouldn't harm a fly even if it bit him. In truth, Jesus was a realist—the Creator of reality—who had an astounding grip of the times and the applicable Law, as well as the nature and sinfulness of man. He was no pansy or bleeding heart like many would seek to portray Him for their own purposes. He grew up to manhood in the town of Nazareth in northern Israel, the son of Joseph the carpenter and his wife Mary. As documented earlier, both of his earthly parents were descendants of King David according to the flesh. We who accept the Holy Bible as the inerrant Word of God know that Jesus Christ was, in reality, God in human flesh, conceived of the Holy Spirit, and that His incarnated body developed in Mary's womb without inheriting the pervasive sin nature from either of his earthly parents (Luke 1:35).

As the eldest son in that family, certain duties would have been mandatory in any Orthodox Jewish household. It is highly probable that Jesus was required, after He came of age, to actually *kill* the Passover lamb, an annual ritual in those times, which required a pilgrimage to Jerusalem. We will discuss this further below.

In doing research for this book, I ran across a number of vegetarian sites which point to one of the Old Testament's prophecies about the

Messiah, of which there are many specific ones. The one most quoted by vegetarians is Isaiah 7:14-15. The first verse indicates that Jesus Christ would be born of a virgin and would be called Immanuel, in Hebrew meaning "God with us." This particular verse is doubtless Messianic, since Christ fulfilled both these requirements. These vegetarians claim, however, that the next verse also applies to Christ. Many prophecies have a double meaning or a partial application, and sometimes a bit of discernment is needed to tell exactly what is Messianic and what applies only to a current situation addressed by the prophet. Isaiah 7:15 states, "He will eat curds and honey at the time He knows enough to refuse evil and choose good." Some hold the view that Christ did take these foods as a child, so the verse applies partially to Him, but this doubtless would not have been His only food.

Many Bible scholars agree that this verse and the next one apply only to the then-current situation in Israel and not to the future Messiah.[1, 2] This seems to be the prevailing view because these two verses obviously allude to military and political intrigue surrounding Judah's King Ahaz, ruler of Southern Israel when Isaiah wrote the prophecy. An alliance had been formed between the king's two main enemies: the Northern Kingdom of Israel, and Aram, which is modern Syria. The next verse indicates "before the boy will know enough to refuse evil and choose good, the land whose two kings you dread will be forsaken." The curds and honey thus may not refer to Christ at all, because His diet was quite obviously standard for His time, plus He *always* refused evil and chose good. The prophecy thus must apply to an actual child born to the prophet Isaiah, a youngster Isaiah predicted would be thrust into a very unstable and difficult national situation at about the time he came of age. Because of the scarcity of usual foods, he would eat curds and honey, the food of nomads. The view that these verses apply only to that time is backed up by Isaiah 8:3, where Isaiah "approached the prophetess, and she conceived." Thus the child in Isaiah 7:15 is an actual child born to Isaiah's wife, who was apparently a virgin until that point, and *not* the future Messiah. Verse 7:14 applies to both that child and to Jesus Christ, with "Immanuel" being merely the proper name of Isaiah's child, but literally describing Jesus Christ. Others, including Matthew

Henry and John Calvin, indicate that Jesus may have eaten such as a part of his diet as a child.[3, 4] child. Either way, vegans can't make much of verse 7:15. Even if it did apply to Jesus Christ, both curds and honey are animal products!

The Passover lamb was an important part of the annual observation, and a perfect specimen was selected by each Jewish family five days before it was slain, which coincides in timing to Jesus' triumphal entry into Jerusalem, offering Himself to Israel five days before He was sacrificed on the cross. This lamb lived with the family in their temporary pilgrimage shelter, and was treated with utmost attention and respect; much like one would care for a pet. Killing the lamb could be performed by a layman, which Jesus was, not being descended from the priestly tribe of Levi, though the blood had to be caught by one of the priests.[5] We will discuss this further below. After the Passover lamb was killed, every member of the family was required to eat at least a small piece of the lamb before the family finished the meal.[6] There is no conceivable way that Jesus could have avoided this requirement to eat red meat.

Some have alleged that they can't envision that Jesus would kill. They need to read the Book of Revelation, where Jesus slays innumerable godless human beings with tools so incredible few people could have thought of them (His mouth-held sword, Revelation 19:21, and fire from heaven, Revelation 20:9). These extraordinary methods and tools actually add credence to the God-inspired nature of the Scriptures because of the unlikelihood such events would be included in any manmade religion. Yes, Jesus has killed, can easily kill, and will kill again, but all in complete righteousness. Since He is the Creator incarnate (John 1:3; Colossians 1:16), it is His privilege to give life and to take it according to His divine justice. To suppose that He would do the first but refrain from the second is a grave misunderstanding.

In the same way, heaping criticism on a butcher because he slaughters a cow or pig is a great error. The butcher, the sheep or cattle rancher, the chicken farmer, the hunter, the tanner, and people of many other such professions or avocations, are made in the image of God and are engaged in normal, God-sanctioned activities. Man kills because he was designed with the ability to kill, and animals were put on earth for man's service, which, after the flood of Noah, included taking some for food and other uses. The only sin involved in killing an animal is by doing it in an intentionally inhumane or inefficient fashion so the animal suffers unnecessarily, or by illegal or unethical means in violation of human laws or, as explained earlier, killing for simple sport and leaving the carcass to rot—a waste of the animal's life. A sure ramification of the Biblical mandate to be good stewards is that profligate waste, such as that perpetrated on the American bison in the late 1800s, is to be condemned as counter to God's ordinances. The ethical butcher, the practiced hunter who provides sustenance for his family, and the efficient livestock farmer are the epitome of people doing what God has ordained that they do.

Since Jesus is the only person in history to keep the Law of Moses perfectly, He had to do certain things. One was to comply with all the rules and regulations related to festivals and feasts mandated by the Law. As previously mentioned, perhaps the most important one of these is Passover, which is still observed today. It is celebrated by Jews in remembrance of their escape from Egyptian bondage more than three thousand years ago, and it is celebrated by Christians because it accurately foretold the coming Messiah, many details pertaining to His death, and other facts pertinent to His resurrection. It also is a major part of Easter, which commemorates the death and then the bodily resurrection of Christ after His crucifixion, the most important events in all of history. As the apostle Paul states from 1 Corinthians 15:12-19, "if there is no resurrection of the dead, not even Christ has been raised...and if Christ has not been raised, your faith is worthless; you are still in your sins" (verses 13, 17).

It is interesting to contemplate the parallels between Christ our Passover and the sacrificial lamb of the Jewish Passover. The Passover lamb had to be a male without blemish or imperfection of any kind (Leviticus 23:12); it had to be sacrificed without breaking any of its bones (Exodus 12:46), and its blood served to cause God's death angel to "pass over" the house where it was sprinkled (Exodus 12:13). The parallels between the Passover lamb and Jesus Christ are far too numerous to list exhaustively here, but suffice it to say Jesus was predicted to be the ultimate sacrifice for the sins of humanity (Isaiah 53).

I emphasize the Passover because, as noted at the opening of this chapter, it was by far the most important Jewish holiday in Jesus' time on earth, and it accurately predicted what would happen to the Messiah when He appeared. Remember, Jesus was not just a practicing Jew; He was a Jew who practiced the Law perfectly. Had He failed in even one minor point, His sacrifice for all of mankind would have been insufficient to pay for sin. However, we find that God the Father proclaimed Him to be "My beloved Son, with whom I am well-pleased" (Matthew 17:5). Moreover, He raised Jesus from the dead, one of the most provable facts in all of history even if one goes on the literary evidence alone.[7] Jesus couldn't have avoided participating in the Passover celebration, even had He managed to evade having to kill the Passover lamb (an act to which He would doubtless have had no aversion anyway). He would have had to complete the Passover meal, which consisted primarily of roasted lamb (Exodus 12:8-10). We have specific confirmation that Jesus ate the Passover meal with His inner circle of disciples in Luke 22:8. I am certain that meat was a normal part of His diet, as it was for every other human being on the planet at that time.

I also firmly believe that Jesus personally killed the Passover lamb, probably on multiple occasions. The original Passover in Egypt was celebrated in individual homes (Exodus 12:3-11), but after the temple was built in Jerusalem, Jews were specifically required to make a pilgrimage there in order to celebrate the Passover, as described in Deuteronomy 16:5-7. Remember, Jesus lived as a carpenter in Nazareth until He was about thirty years old, when His public ministry began (Luke 3:23), and He went through many celebrations of Passover. We have a record of one of his pilgrimages to Jerusalem at age twelve, found in Luke 2:41-51. Significantly, there is never any mention of Joseph, His earthly father, after this incident when Jesus was twelve years old.

It appears likely that Joseph had died by the time Jesus was a young adult, after which he became the oldest male in His earthly family. The Scriptures are silent as to exactly who was to kill the lamb for each Jewish family group if it wasn't sacrificed by a priest. In such an occurrence, it is reasonable to assume that the duty would fall to the eldest male member of the family, which would have been Jesus in this case. Again the Scriptures do not tell us who sacrificed the Passover lamb for the "Last Supper" that Jesus celebrated with His disciples, but there is absolutely no room for doubt that a lamb was killed. Luke 22:8-13 tells us that Jesus sent the disciples to a predetermined place where they prepared the Passover meal. In this incident, either a priest at the temple or one of the disciples slit the throat of the lamb before it was roasted. This incident also serves to confirm that the Passover celebration did not have to occur in the temple itself, even though the actual sacrifice of the lamb had to take place there.

Additionally, failing to participate in the mandated sacrifice would have left Jesus with an incomplete experience as a keeper of the Law. Sacrificing the Passover lamb was accomplished by slitting the lamb's throat and draining its blood, which I'm sure Jesus did expertly, cleanly, and painlessly. Since God had already taken the lives of innocent animals to cover Adam and Eve after their original sin, both physically and spiritually, God incarnate would have no problem participating fully in the same type of somber ceremony that involved killing an innocent lamb to provide a temporary sin-covering for His earthly family. It must have been an awesome feeling for Christ to know that He personally was destined to be sacrificed, and that such was His prime mission to the world, in fact.

Even if Jesus left the duty of killing the Passover lamb to the priests during the annual feast, killing animals for food was a normal part of daily life for Jews during Jesus' earthly life. There was no refrigeration in those days, so all meat had to be consumed within a short time after it was sacrificed. As noted before, the need for regular "secular" sacrifice of animals in places remote from the central worship place is covered in Deuteronomy 12:15-27, and it is highly probable that this duty fell to the eldest son on many occasions. As the perfect son to his parents, it is hard to envision how Jesus could have escaped this routine duty.

Use It All, Brother!

We have already covered the Scripture (Mark 7:14-19) where Jesus declared all food to be "clean," including any animal a person is inclined to eat. During the time that Christ was bodily present on earth, no natural man knew about the need for vitamin B12, iron, zinc, or amino acids. They ate meat because there was no healthful alternative for them. I believe Jesus declared all meat to be "clean" to facilitate evangelizing Gentiles and to fulfill the Law by removing such external prohibitions. Remember, the internal working of the Holy Spirit rather than the outward practice of religious rituals was very soon to become the distinguishing factor of the people of God. This put an end to the keeping of endless lists of dos and don'ts—known then and now as legalism—and replaced ritual observance with internal guidance through the Holy Spirit's work in individual lives. Perhaps Christ even wanted to expand the reach of legitimate good nutrition to as many people as possible, and meat was an essential part of good nutrition. It still is today, unless one takes extreme steps to replace its important health benefits.

When Jesus declared all foods "clean," this was a radical departure from the Law, and actually marked a major turning point in the history of God's people. By this declaration, Jesus freed every person on earth to eat whatever animal he wanted to eat, without regard to hooves, rumination, presence or absence of fins and scales, or any other physical characteristic.

Some have presumed, and even presented flawed evidence, that Jesus was a vegetarian. This is pure baloney. While we have only indirect (though compelling and irrefutable) evidence that Jesus ate red meat, we have direct references to Him eating fish, feeding fish to others, and encouraging fishing. As mentioned, at least six of His disciples were fishermen. Jesus once *commanded* his apostle Peter to go fishing in order to supernaturally obtain a coin to pay their taxes (Matthew 17:27). In at least two instances He fed fish to thousands of people at the same time (Matthew 14:16-21; Matthew 15:32-38).

In Luke 24:41-43, after His resurrection, Jesus asked His disciples directly for something to eat. To quote: "And they gave Him a piece of broiled fish; and He took it and ate it before them." He apparently even went fishing Himself and gave instructions to others as to how to fish. In the account in John 21:9, the resurrected Jesus already had a fire going with fish cooking when the disciples recognized Him on the shore. Just prior to that, He instructed the fishing disciples to change technique a bit, and their net became so filled with fish that it was at the breaking point. It was only after this supernatural occurrence that the apostle Peter recognized Him as the resurrected Christ. The bottom-line conclusion is that there is absolutely no question that Jesus ate meat.

Eating Meat Forever?

There is a far more important lesson in these episodes, however. Jesus was resurrected at that point and was clothed in His permanent, glorified resurrection body, a body that will never die. The apostle John tells us (1 John 3:2) that "it has not appeared as yet what we will be [in our resurrected bodies—brackets mine]. We know that, when He appears, we shall be like Him." Jesus *ate fish* while newly adorned with His supernatural resurrection body; and *we shall be like Him*! Thus even in our eternal state, we will still have the capacity to eat meat! Until the New Heavens and New Earth are a reality, this may be an option we choose to exercise (as God Himself—likely as the pre-incarnate Christ—chose to eat meat during His encounter with Abraham in Genesis 18, as covered in Chapter Four). That precedent was set at least two thousand years before Christ was born into the world as a human baby. In the eternal state, it is probable that even animal death may be abolished and, in that case, eating meat would no longer be a possibility, as we will discuss below.

It even appears possible, and many authorities concur in this, that God's people will be meat-eaters when Christ returns, a possibility mentioned earlier. These scholars cite direct references to fishing under Messiah's rule in Ezekiel 47:9-10, along with continuing sacrifice and consumption of animals found in that same book. Earlier chapters of Ezekiel also refer to sacrifice of animals as part of continued observances of Passover and the Feast of Tabernacles, perhaps by pious future Jews who still haven't recognized Christ for who He is, or possibly as memorials to Christ's ultimate sacrifice on the cross (Ezekiel 43-45). Parts of these animals will be quite eminently edible, and will be consumed by those who make the sacrifices (Ezekiel 44:29), in accordance with guidelines found in the ancient Law of Moses (such as in Exodus 29:32). I can find no Scriptural reason to believe that, as eternal beings housed in resurrection bodies that will never die, we will change our eating habits when we are present bodily with Christ.

This is a good place to note that under the premillennial interpretation of the reign of Christ on earth, humans who survive the tribulation period alive will still have unglorified, unresurrected (natural) bodies, and they will have children, live to old ages, and die (Isaiah 65:20-23). These people still living in "natural" bodies will be unregenerated, and will continue to possess the sin nature, though they apparently will sin infrequently, and it will be judged and punished immediately when they do. Sin will still carry a penalty, as it does today (Isaiah 65:20). Additionally, they will continue with the same dietary needs we have today, and sacrifices such as specified in the Book of Ezekiel will provide the meat they need for optimum health in a perfect kingdom.*

Perhaps the most instructive passage in the Bible about Jesus' attitude toward eating meat is John 6:54-55, where Jesus makes a statement so incredible and difficult to understand that many of His erstwhile followers deserted Him. He states that "He who eats *My* flesh and drinks *My* blood has eternal life, and I will raise him up on the last day. For *My* flesh is true food and *My* blood is true drink." Jesus actually *requires* that we eat His flesh and drink His blood in order to have eternal life! That doesn't sound very vegetarian to me. Christians commemorate the sacrifice of Jesus on the cross by partaking symbolically of His flesh and blood in the serving of communion, or the Lord's Supper, on a regular basis. Spiritually, we take in His flesh and blood by believing in Him and the atoning death He suffered, as well as His bodily resurrection from the dead, and thus receive eternal life.

Jesus Permitted Others to Kill

Jesus had much to say about the worth of a human being as compared to animals. He makes it clear in several passages that a man has immeasurably higher worth than any animal. The passage I cited previously is Matthew 10:29-31, where Jesus states "...do not fear; you are of more value than many sparrows." He repeats the comparison of man's value to that of sparrows in Luke 12:6-7, again stressing how much more valuable a

---

* Postmillennial believers maintain upon the same Scriptures that *all* men, including the regenerate, will remain mortal in the millennial reign, where Christ reigns from the right hand of the Father (Ps. 110). –Ed.

man is than "many sparrows." In Matthew 12:12, Jesus exclaims, "Of how much more value then is a man than a sheep!" The unmistakable lesson is that man, God's image-bearer, is infinitely more valuable than any animal.

Jesus told perhaps hundreds of parables, many of which are recorded in the Gospels. One of the best known is the parable of the prodigal son, found in Luke 15:11-32. In this parable, Jesus twice uses the killing of a fattened calf as the epitome of celebration. In no way does He condemn the killing or eating of the calf, but He clearly endorses the activity by the context. Another story involving meat utilization is found in Matthew 22:4, where Jesus tells the parable of a king who kills oxen and fattened cattle for a wedding feast. That episode certainly presents eating good (and even grain-fed) meat as symbolic of the blessing of being in God's kingdom.

Jesus Used Animals—and Expected Others to Do So

Jesus' mother Mary likely utilized a beast of burden to journey from Nazareth to Bethlehem while she was very nearly full-term with the unborn Jesus (Luke 2), though the method of travel can only be inferred. Shepherds, keepers of domestic sheep, were honored by God when they were called as witnesses by the angels who announced Christ's birth in Bethlehem (Luke 2:8-20). At Jesus' circumcision on the eighth day after His birth, his natural parents took him to the temple in Jerusalem for this rite (Luke 2: 22-24). Because they were poor, they sacrificed a bird on this occasion instead of a lamb, which was the required sacrifice of those with means in order to fulfill the Law of Moses. The poor (as Joseph and Mary were) could sacrifice an inexpensive pigeon or dove (Leviticus 12:3-8).

Jesus Himself also used beasts of burden. It was predicted by the prophet Zechariah (Zechariah 9:9) that the Messiah would present Himself as King to the nation of Israel "mounted on a donkey, even on a colt, the foal of a donkey." This was fulfilled in the Gospels when He sent the disciples to get a donkey on which no one had ever ridden, and then He used it for what is generally referred to as the "triumphal entry" into Jerusalem on the day we now call Palm Sunday (Matthew 21:2-7), a week before Easter Sunday.

The closest associate of Jesus early in His ministry was his cousin (according to the flesh), John the Baptist. John was sent to announce the coming of the King, and to preach a baptism of repentance for the forgiveness of sins. Of special note for purposes of this book is Matthew 3:4, which describes the clothing John wore (made of camel's hair with a leather belt) and the food he ate (locusts—a kind of grasshopper; and wild honey, made by bees). All these are animal products. Had Jesus had the slightest bent in favor of animal rights of any kind, He could never have stated after John's imprisonment, "Truly I say to you, among those born of women there has not arisen anyone greater than John the Baptist" (Matthew 11:11).

Think about the Future

Premillennialist theologians believe that Christ's reign on earth will serve to show that God's plan for Planet Earth can and will be fulfilled with Christ as King ruling with absolute righteousness and justice from Jerusalem. Under that widely held system of theology, the utter depravity of man in his unredeemed state will be demonstrated when Satan is loosed from his thousand-year confinement, an imprisonment that starts just before the Kingdom begins (Revelation 20:2-3). Premillennialists believe that, despite perfect living conditions for a full millennium, when Satan is freed "for a time," his demonic forces and the natural people (millions of descendants of survivors of the tribulation endured under the Beast a thousand years earlier) will follow him in large numbers, though the rebellion will be quickly crushed (Revelation 20:7-10).

If indeed this turns out to be the correct interpretation, vegetarians and animal rights activists may still find some comfort in a couple of points. During Christ's reign, there apparently will be no adversarial relationship between animals such as exists between predator and prey at this time, at least not in the vicinity of Jerusalem. Isaiah 65:25 states clearly, "The wolf and the lamb will graze together, and the lion will eat straw like the ox; and dust will be the serpent's food [the curse of Genesis 3:14 will still remain on the snake—brackets mine]. They will do no evil or harm *in all My holy mountain*." I've used italics to emphasize that an adversarial, predator-prey relationship could continue to exist elsewhere.

Additionally, in the final state of the New Heavens and the New Earth, all human beings could revert to being vegetarians, as God originally intended. Revelation 21:4 indicates there will be no more death at that time. At the very least this means no human death—it isn't stated whether animals could still die, though I believe they will not, since animal death is also the result of man's original sin. Revelation 22:2 points out the tree of life, which will bear twelve kinds of fruit (a different one each month), and the leaves of which will be "for the healing of the nations." I'm sure all these will be rich sources of the nutrients we are now forced to get from animals, if indeed we still need these. Revelation 22:3 indicates the curse (over sin, which led originally to death) will also be gone. Unless a person believes God's Word is true, however, they won't be there to enjoy the change back to our original diet.

Regardless of whether my specific thoughts on these matters turn out to be correct, it is abundantly clear that Jesus had no problem with animal utilization of all types. At His Second Coming, He will be *riding a white horse* (Revelation 19:11), as will all the armies of Heaven who return with Him (Revelation 19:14). If anyone has a problem with utilizing horses for transportation, they certainly can't support it with the Word of God.

To suppose that Jesus had a special relationship to animals that put Him at odds with the culture of the day is improbable speculation. Scripture leaves no doubt that He ate meat and fish, used positive examples about eating meat, encouraged fishing, perhaps fished Himself, and definitely utilized beasts of burden. By His recorded words and by what He didn't say, He approved all forms of animal utilization. Animal sacrifices will apparently continue even when all Kingdom promises have been fulfilled, according to Ezekiel 45 and 46, and some of the meat of these animals will be consumed (Ezekiel 44:29). There will be fishing and consumption of fish when Jesus reigns, according to Ezekiel 47. Jesus was certainly by no means a vegetarian or an animal rights advocate. To believe otherwise is to believe a lie.

Notes

1 Charles Pfeiffer, *The Wycliffe Bible Commentary*, Moody Press, Nineteenth printing, 1981, 618.

2 John Walvoord and Roy Zuck, *The Bible Knowledge Commentary* (Old Testament), Victor Books, Fourth printing, 1987, 1047-1048.

3 Matthew Henry, *Matthew Henry Commentary on the Whole Bible*, (Nashville, TN: Thomas Nelson, 1979), "The Book of the Prophet Isaiah," 19.

4 John Calvin, *Calvin's Commentaries, Volume VII* (Grand Rapids, MI: Baker Book House, 1996), 249.

5 www.jewishencyclopedia.com/view.jsp?artid=99&letter=P, "Passover Sacrifice," [accessed February 2009].

6 Mishnah in tractate Pesachim, chapters 5 through 10, *The Scottenstein Edition, Talmud Bavli*, Artscroll Series.

7 Josh McDowell, *Evidence That Demands a Verdict*, (Nashville, TN: Thomas Nelson, 1992).

NINE

New Testament Animal Utilization Apart from The Four Gospels

Books and articles I have read proposing that Jesus Christ, and indeed God the Father, holds a bias in favor of animal rights typically stop with the Gospels. While such arguments are very adequately refuted by the Gospels alone as outlined in the previous chapter, the rest of the New Testament also clearly negates the empty premise of animal rights and animal equality. In this chapter are numerous examples.

Not Only Jesus Approved Animal Utilization

The apostle Paul wrote much of the New Testament, and he is so clear on animal utilization and meat eating that I'm not surprised he is mostly discounted as a source of animal rights propaganda. Paul ate meat and encouraged others to do so, and so did practically every other writer in this section of the Bible. There is also reference to additional kinds of animal utilization, such as tanning hides for clothing and other uses (Simon the tanner hosted the apostle Peter for a time, as recorded in Acts 10:6). In this same chapter (Acts 10:13) is the section already covered earlier, where Peter was commanded by God to "Get up, Peter, kill and eat!" This incident is related again by Peter to his fellow disciples in Acts 11:7.

The apostle Paul was a tent maker by trade, a business that dealt primarily in animal skins. He actively practiced this trade for financial support far into his career as a traveling evangelist (Acts 18:3).

A more subtle reference to utilizing animals by a Christian after the Gospels is found in Acts 23:24, where Paul is provided a mount for his journey from Jerusalem to Caesarea. He didn't protest the means of transportation by horseback in the least, nor does he mention it later in his writings as being wrong. In a later chapter of this same book (Acts 28:3-4), Paul is bitten by a viper, which he kills by shaking it off his hand into the fire. In neither of these instances are the involved animals attributed any "rights," and indeed the subject never comes up.

After the Jerusalem Council in Acts 15, Gentile (non-Jewish) Christians were sent a letter advising them to "abstain from things sacrificed to idols and from blood and from things strangled" (Acts 15:29). This would have been an ideal time to advise them not to eat meat at all, had that been God's intent for man. The omission is obviously an endorsement of eating meat that isn't sacrificed to idols or strangled (the latter of which would have prevented draining the creature's blood when it was killed). That this referred to *animals* sacrificed to idols is further confirmed in Acts 21:25, where the word "meat" is specified.

I have read the argument by vegans that it is impossible to eat meat without getting a little blood along with the meat, the implication being that eating any meat at all violates this command. There is indeed microscopic evidence of blood in any meat if one examines it under adequate magnification, even when the blood has been drained, but this information was not available to mankind when this order was given. Obviously God knew well about this tiny residual, so what is intended in the commandment not to eat blood is this: Do not purposely eat blood or meat from which visible blood has not been drained. Additionally, as I mentioned above, had all meat been disqualified by the technicality that a few red blood cells are still present in it, changing the command to "don't eat any meat at all" would have naturally followed. The fact that such did not occur is highly significant.

One of the most telling passages in the Bible regarding consumption of animal flesh is found in Romans 14. This whole chapter is devoted to food, and specifically to meat. If one uses a modern translation, the word for "meat" can be translated in the Bible as the more generic word "food," so one must be careful interpreting any passage that states simply "meat" or "food." Generally the word "meat" in a modern translation means what it says: animal flesh. As I mentioned in the Introduction, in the King James Version the word "meat" is used freely in the opposite sense, that is, as an alternative term for food or meals in general.

Pertinent parts of this chapter of Romans are in verses 1-4, where the one who eats only vegetables is called "weak." This would certainly include a weakness of faith (verse 1) but, in those days, such a person would also have been physically weak due to malnutrition, unless God somehow supernaturally provided them nutrition as He had for the prophet Daniel when he was a young captive in Babylon, as described in Daniel 1.

While some truly gifted athletes who abstain from meat are touted by vegetarian propagandists as the epitome of fitness because of their vegetarianism,[1] most of these athletes are not vegans at all, but consume eggs and dairy products. Those who do not must adhere carefully to a complicated regimen of supplements to avoid nutritional deficiency because it has been recognized for more than a century that meat-eaters, in general, have superior strength, endurance, and adaptability to changing environments than strict vegetarians.[2] One must wonder what spectacular feats these very special vegetarian athletes might have accomplished had they eaten a more balanced diet. Furthermore, many experts agree that some animal products are important to overall health, especially in pregnant women and growing children, but also in the average adult.[3] Linkage of vegetarianism to various nutritional deficiency illnesses is the norm in the medical literature[4, 5, 6] as well as in medical practice.

The passage from Romans above has specific application to the animal rights movement, since that deviant philosophy consistently criticizes humans eating animals. Note that it goes on to state, "The one who eats [meat] is not to regard with contempt the one who does not eat, and the one who does not eat [meat] is not to judge the one who eats, for God has accepted him" (14:3) [brackets mine]. As one source puts it, "The one who ate was not to be constantly despising the one who did not eat. The one who did not eat was not to be constantly condemning the one who did. The eating of certain foods for the Christian is not in itself a moral matter."[7] It is clear, then, that no one gains favor in God's eyes or elevates his or her spiritual position by abstaining from eating meat.

We omnivores should not criticize vegetarians because they eat no meat; it would be a sin to do so. On the other hand, it is clearly also a sin for vegetarians to criticize anyone for eating meat. My intention is to offer no criticism of those who choose a vegetarian diet; on the other hand, it is quite fair to offer observations of where they are obviously in error, and to refute the misinformation that it is wrong for *me* to be unashamed of my utilization of animals in myriad ways, including as food.

It is also quite clear, however, that Romans 14 is not in actuality about strict vegetarians versus omnivorous people at all. It is undeniable, in view of later admonitions about eating meat sacrificed to idols, that these were new believers who abstained from meat only because they couldn't be *certain* it hadn't been sacrificed to an idol before the carcass showed up in the meat market.[8] Mature believers were free to eat any meat with a clear conscience, but they were not to risk causing new or untaught believers to violate their conscience by having them eat meat of unknown origin. The apostle Paul elaborates on this key principle in verses 13-23. The principle of not causing a weaker brother or sister (usually new or untaught believers in Christ) to stumble is further elaborated in later books of the New Testament.

Paul discusses the eating of meat in more detail in the next book of the Bible after Romans. In 1 Corinthians 3:2 he states, "I gave you milk to drink, not solid food; for you were not yet able to receive it." He is speaking of spiritual growth, but he uses the metaphor of food as an illustration. Babies require milk, whether they are physical babies or spiritual babies (new or untaught believers in Christ). Mature individuals can receive food, physical or spiritual, that requires more digestion. It's a great way to explain the nature of spiritual growth, and Paul does not hesitate to refer to "solid food" without excluding meat. Neither did the writer of Hebrews, as covered below when he wrote on the same topic.

In 1 Corinthians 8:4-13, Paul further clarifies eating meat sacrificed to idols. He minimizes the importance of where the meat originated by stating there really isn't anything to an idol, anyway, because there is only one true God. He goes on to say that some people (likely immature Christians) have their consciences violated if they knowingly eat meat sacrificed to an idol. Verse 8 is key: "Food will not commend us to God; we are neither the worse if we do not eat, nor the better if we do eat." By "food" Paul obviously means meat, since that is what the chapter is about, and it is specified as meat in verse 13. He goes on to reaffirm the principle that love is to predominate, a concept he expands later, and which I will address shortly. The love connection is that one is not to risk causing a weaker brother to stumble (violate their conscience) when a mature Christian exercises his God-given freedom in this area, basically the same idea as found in Romans 14. One is free to eat meat of any kind from any source so long as it doesn't cause an immature believer to violate his conscience by eating meat that might have been sacrificed to an idol. This "weaker brother" simply hasn't grown to the point of understanding the degree of freedom they have in this area, and the fact that an idol to a Christian is no different from any other inanimate object, and holds no power over any area of life.

A distinctly different slant is presented in the following chapter. In 1 Corinthians 9:7-9, Paul asks "Who tends a flock and does not use the milk of the flock?" He obviously approves of the practice. He then repeats the Old Testament principle of not muzzling the ox while it is threshing, justly allowing the animal to enjoy some of the fruit of its labor, as covered earlier. As stated before, God's concern for the welfare of oxen pales in comparison to concern for His image-bearer. Most Christian churches apply this principle of "not muzzling the ox" to their leaders, especially the pastor, who is deserving of a salary in exchange for carrying out his duties.

In 1 Corinthians 10:25-31, Paul further elucidates the idea of eating meat sacrificed to idols. In verse 25, he states plainly to the person with no complicating issues such as an observing weaker brother: "Eat anything that is sold in the meat market without asking questions for conscience' sake." He then addresses the issue of eating meat when invited to another's home, again telling believers not to question where the meat originated. However, if a believer is informed the meat was sacrificed to an idol without even asking the question, they are not to eat it. To do so is to ignore the principle of love by possibly violating the informer's conscience, even though you yourself are free to eat the meat. In today's world, meat sacrificed to idols is not much of a concern, so purchasing and eating meat in modern times holds few potential problems such as existed in Paul's time.

In a later book (Colossians 2:16-17), the apostle Paul states that Christians should let no one "act as your judge in regard to food or drink …things which are a mere shadow of what is to come; but the substance belongs to Christ." In this way, he tells us that the old restraints of the Law of Moses have been removed, especially concerning clean and unclean animals. There were no restrictions regarding the eating of vegetables in the Law, so we know that this liberation pertaining to food applies *exclusively* to meat. As for drink, this could possibly apply to alcoholic beverages, though wine was almost universally accepted in Paul's time, and the only inviolable rule Christians had to follow was not to get drunk (Ephesians 5:18). Even today most Christians are free to drink alcoholic beverages in moderation without violating their conscience so long as they don't become inebriated; however, to some, such drinks are the devil's brew in any quantity. This is an area where the same principle of love is more pertinent in our time, in that a Christian who has the freedom to drink alcoholic beverages should do so in a manner that doesn't violate the conscience of the believer who hasn't this freedom, for whatever reason.

Like Paul in 1 Corinthians 3, the author of the book of Hebrews refers to both milk and solid food in his dissertation on Christian spiritual growth. In Hebrews 5:12-14 it is stated, "For though by this time you ought to be teachers, you have need again for someone to teach you the elementary principles of the oracles of God, and you have come to need milk and not solid food. For everyone who partakes only of milk is not accustomed to the word of righteousness, for he is an infant. But solid food is for the mature, who because of practice have their senses trained to discern good and evil."

Clearly, here is another author of Holy Scripture who was accustomed to seeing babies physically drink milk and older people physically eat meat and other solid foods, and he offers criticism only to those who have not made the transition in spiritual terms. Note that the outcome of becoming able to eat and digest solid food is the ability to distinguish good from evil, a characteristic known in Christian lingo as "discernment." It is highly significant that possessing this desirable quality is represented by the eating and unhindered digestion of solid food, while the converse is true of those still limited to consumption of milk. Either way, though, by not specifically excluding meat in his instructions, the author gives his blessing to two unabashed forms of animal utilization that are reprehensible to hardcore animal rights advocates (eating meat and drinking milk). As always, both are presented in Scripture as typical, normal, and eminently acceptable.

Still in the book of Hebrews, we find the essential principle that "without shedding of blood there is no forgiveness" of sins (Hebrews 9:22). Jesus Christ shed His own blood as final payment for man's sin for all who will believe, so we don't need to sacrifice animals in order to temporarily cover our sins in this Christian era. As noted earlier, the book of Ezekiel in the Old Testament strongly suggests that memorial sacrifices of animals will be made in some form of reconstructed temple when Christ reigns bodily on earth from Jerusalem. Such sacrifices would in no way supplement or improve the completed and totally sufficient sacrifice of Christ, however, but could be a formal way of remembering that awesome eternal event. For any who would forget or minimize the significance of the cross and the resurrection, I would point out a later verse: "It is a terrifying thing to fall into the hands of the living God" (Hebrews 10:31), and "our God is a consuming fire" (Hebrews 12:29). Both these truths are inevitable realities for all who reject Christ and His sacrifice. As C. S. Lewis wrote in *The Chronicles of Narnia*, God isn't safe. But He is good.

Not Only as Physical Food

The book of James was written by the earthly brother of Jesus (the natural son of Jesus' father and mother, Joseph and Mary), who became a leader of the first-century church in Jerusalem. In it, he offers several interesting references to animal utilization. In James 3:3, he refers to using a bit in the mouth of horses to direct them. By this, he illustrates that the tongue needs direction in a similar way. In no way does he criticize the age-old practice of using horses and training them to do man's will.

In that same chapter (verse 7), James states that "every species of beasts and birds, of reptiles and creatures of the sea, is tamed, and has been tamed by the human race." He is, of course, referring to all known creatures, and the "taming" would be exercising dominion by either capturing these creatures for food, turning them into working animals, or even by making them pets where appropriate. Animal rights types, of course, are opposed to all forms of utilization that James rightly sees as simple application of God-ordained dominion.

We have established in earlier chapters that the fisherman and eminent apostle Peter had no problem with animal utilization, and practiced it regularly both before and after Jesus' sacrificial death on the cross. Peter wrote two books of the New Testament, 1 Peter and 2 Peter. In both these books, there is positive reference to continued animal utilization. In 1 Peter 2:2, he uses the metaphor of "pure milk" for the new Christian's experience of growth by studying the Holy Scriptures. In verse 25 of that same chapter, he uses the image of straying sheep to picture believers who commit sin, and then likens Jesus "the Shepherd and Guardian of your souls." In no manner does Peter criticize herding or utilization of domestic sheep, and instead builds his positive instructions around them.

In this same book of 1 Peter, it states in verse 5:8 that "Your adversary, the devil, prowls around like a roaring lion, seeking someone to devour." The apostle is obviously referring to the spiritual danger that exists in the world because of demonic activity; however, I believe this spiritual battle will one day become a physical reality, a fact we will later explore in depth.

In 2 Peter 2:10-12, one verse of which we have covered earlier, people who "indulge the flesh in its corrupt desires and despise authority" are compared to "unreasoning animals, born as creatures of instinct to be captured and killed." Such people revile "where they have no knowledge," and "will in the destruction of those creatures also be destroyed." Note that this verse cannot in any way be applied to the herders of cattle, sheep, or goats, or to the poultry farmer, hunter, butcher, medical researcher, pet owner, or other animal user who lives a humble, godly lifestyle and submits themselves to the authority of the Holy Scriptures. It applies only to the self-willed and rebellious who refuse to acknowledge God and His

Word as sovereign and supreme, and ultimately to all who revel in their deception and reject Jesus Christ as Lord (1 John 2:22-26).

Misguided Hate

It is not at all surprising that the animal rights movement has little regard for what consequences their actions have on populations of animals (other than predators, which are unquestionably their elite project and which have a special role to play for the ultimate Antichrist, the Beast of Revelation). Their only goal is to short-circuit God-ordained human utilization of animals, even if it takes terrorist acts, devastation of people and resources, and piles of dead animals to accomplish this. Some of these terrorist acts, such as the June 7, 2007, attack on a mink farm in Boyers, Pennsylvania, have resulted in massive animal casualties, and many have involved property losses of millions of dollars. There have been more than a hundred documented attacks on law-abiding animal operations between January 2007 and March 2008, and about fifteen hundred more over the past decade.[9]

Besides known terrorist acts by animal rights activists, there are increasing numbers of more damaging incidents of suspected terrorism, such as the *e. coli* contamination of 25 million pounds of ground beef at Hudson Foods in 1997 and 18.6 million pounds at ConAgra in 2002, costing both food giants millions of dollars that ultimately is passed on to consumers. An even more staggering disaster was the contamination of 27.4 million pounds of turkey and chicken deli meats at Pilgrim's Pride in 2002, because of linkage to an outbreak of *Listeria monocytogenes* in the northeastern USA that killed 23 people. However, none of these incidents can be listed as confirmed animal rights terrorist acts because so far no one has been able to prove such a relationship.

Public safety necessitates that meat processing and distribution companies (and in fact all food processors, in view of the anti-human nature of many of these extremist groups) maintain an impeccable level of security, including careful screening of all employees for any hint of a radical animal rights connection. I personally believe simply being a strict vegetarian (vegan) should disqualify a person from working in a meat processing facility. At the very least, a worker's personal food habits and any affiliation with known animal rights terrorist groups should be investigated and documented before they are hired.

Almost all such terrorist incidents, interestingly, have occurred in the USA and Western Europe. I believe 2 Peter 2:10-12 specifically applies to persons who would carry out this kind of destructive anti-human, anti-civilization activity. The entire scenario of animal rights terrorism is, in fact, apocalyptic.

Terrorism is apparently an accepted policy of radical animal rights groups such as People for the Ethical Treatment of Animals (PETA). To quote Bruce Friedrich, PETA's vice president for its International Grassroots Campaign, "If we really believe that animals have the same right to be free from pain and suffering at our hands, then of course we're going to be blowing things up and smashing windows…I think it's a great way to bring animal liberation, considering the level of suffering, the atrocities. I think it would be great if all of the fast-food outlets, slaughterhouses, these laboratories, and banks that fund them, exploded tomorrow." [10, 11] Because of such statements, PETA shows every evidence of being a bona fide terrorist organization with a blatant disregard for human *and* animal life. The American public must demand that they and like groups be investigated as potential terrorists and, where appropriate, prosecuted to the full extent of the law. I will have more analysis of PETA in the following chapter.

One more reference is pertinent to this discussion, and should be repeated regarding the animal rights movement at every opportunity. "It is important to answer the madman. It is important because, left unanswered, his lies and his malice can poison the climate. They can do worse. They can make other men mad. Left unanswered for long enough, they can nourish everything in men and women that is hateful and destructive and murderous. Our end is to ensure that every time the madman shouts in the market place, he is answered." This insightful statement is attributed to the Honorable Roy McMurtry, Attorney General of Ontario.[12] I can only pray that this book is one significant answer to the mad men and women in our society and the world at large.

Real Love and Real Sin

Two more general points must be made before we move on. First, we need to explain love as it is found in the Bible. Love is a major part of God's essence and identity that comes fully into focus only in the New Testament (1 John 4:7-5:3). Christians are the only people in the world who can consistently practice real, self-denying, self-sacrificing love, because Christians are the only ones who possess the ultimate manifestation of God's love, Jesus Christ, living within them in the person of the Holy Spirit. We have already quoted John 3:16, which is a familiar statement to most Christians, which shows that God's infinite love for His image-bearers sent His Son Jesus Christ into the world to offer Himself as the only sufficient sacrifice for sinners, so that whoever believes in Him receives eternal life. That Jesus Christ is God incarnate is made clear in the Gospel of John (John 1:1-3), which states, "In the beginning was the Word, and the Word was with God, and the Word was God (cultic translations that render these last two words as 'became God,' thus denying Christ's deity from eternity past, are a highly unlikely stretch of the Greek original text). He was in the beginning with God. All things came into being by Him, and apart from Him nothing came into being that has come into being." Jesus is not only the eternal Creator God in human flesh, He is the Person of the Holy Trinity that accomplished the act of creation. John goes on to explain "And the Word became flesh and dwelt among us.... No man has seen God at any time; the only begotten God who is in the bosom of the Father, He has explained Him" (verses 14 and 18).

This means that not only is Jesus one with God from eternity past to eternity future, but also He and the apostles He trained who wrote the New Testament have explained all we can know about God in this life. We can learn more about Him, of course, through obedience and trusting Him with our life experiences, but all such learning is based solidly on the already-revealed Word of God.

We know that God is love, and Jesus is the ultimate expression of that love. Religion is man's attempt to reach God; only Jesus Christ is God reaching down to helpless man. There is no other way to know God except through Jesus Christ. This exclusivity claim isn't my idea, either.

It is spelled out unmistakably on the pages of the Bible. John 14:6 is only one of many such passages, where Jesus states plainly and unmistakably, "I am the way, and the truth, and the life; no one comes to the Father, but through Me."

Now as to the word love, it is misused by animal rights activists in every dissertation I have read from their camp that addresses the issue. In 1 John 4:7-5:3, there is further explanation of the nature of God's love, which is a special, self-sacrificing love (translated in the New Testament from the Greek word *agape*). There is also a brotherly love that is often used in the Bible (*phileo* in Greek).

Nowhere in the Bible does it say that human beings should *love* animals in the sense of either of these words. The word *love* in general, in fact, *never* applies in the Bible to the human-animal relationship. The nearest example to a Biblical love relationship between a person and an animal is found in the condemning illustration the prophet Nathan described about a poor man's lamb to King David in 2 Samuel 12, after David's adultery with Bathsheba. Even there, however, the word love is never used and, in any case, the story is obviously metaphorical of the relationship between a man (Uriah) and his wife (Bathsheba).

It is exceedingly clear that we are to love *other people*, and doubtless we are free to hold a form of deep affection for our pets and any other animal, as did the poor man in the story noted above. We can also hold that kind of warmth even for a job or hobby we choose. I believe that love for animals should be recognized for what it is: A temporary relationship, however meaningful it might be in this life. But if we fail to love *other people*, that is a truly serious offense in God's eyes. We are missing the opportunity to develop an eternal relationship with another human being and to demonstrate that we are privileged to show God's love to one of His image-bearers.

Examine this passage from 1 John in detail. God loved us; therefore, we ought to love *one another*. If we love one another, God abides in us and is perfected in us. The one who abides in love abides in God and God is in him. If someone says he loves God yet he hates *his brother*, he is a liar. The one who says he loves God should prove the fact by loving *his brother* also. We love God not by loving some far-away deity that we can't see, touch, or feel—as if God needed such, anyway (He needs nothing whatsoever to be complete within Himself—Acts 17:25). We show our love for God by loving His children and keeping His commandments, among which loving other people is foremost.

Jesus Himself said (Matthew 22:37-40) that the greatest commandment is to love God, and the next greatest is to love your neighbor (not your dog) as much as you do yourself. Never is there any indication whatsoever that this love relationship is between any beings except God and people. Animals are never mentioned, and this is because they don't fit into the picture as part of an *agape* love relationship. Only God is capable of the kind of *agape* love that sent Christ to the cross, and He imparts that love to His followers by a work of the Holy Spirit in individual believers. I myself have had dozens of dogs and cats over the years, and a great affection often develops between master and pet. I have personally shed tears and felt the devastation of losing a dear pet, and the form of sorrow it brings. There cannot be sin in grieving for a time over a lost pet. However, animals are driven by complicated and inexplicable instincts, given to them as part of God's creative will, and certainly there is no Biblical or scientific evidence to prove whether they harbor genuine love.

On the contrary, we are given a somber warning in 1 John 2:15, where it states, "Do not love the world or the things in the world. If anyone loves the world, the love of the Father is not in him." The things of the world *must not* take precedent over eternal things. To deeply love something temporary to the *exclusion* of the eternal is futility at best and, for the Christian, it is sin. I'm certain it's okay with God to have a deep affection for your home, your farm, your pets, your job, and the like. You can even have a form of love for the cattle, sheep, pigs, chickens, or goats under your care. How many times have you heard a person say innocently, "I just love my new job," or "I love working in my garden"? However, to love any of these worldly things more than your human neighbor is clearly contrary to God's will. To do so is a form of materialism that God condemns as "love for the world." This is the point made unmistakably by Jesus Christ Himself when He was asked to name the greatest commandment in Matthew 22.

Second, there are numerous "sin lists" in the New Testament (1 Peter 4:3,15; Galatians 5:19-21; 1 Corinthians 6:9-10; 2 Corinthians 12:20; and Jude 1:16, to inventory a few). None of these catalogs a single sin against animals. In fact, none of the original Ten Commandments addresses a sin against animals, only against God or other people. Of course, it is possible to sin in one's treatment of animals by grossly abusing them, as covered in the Law of Moses. You can also sin against God regarding the environment by willfully polluting it, not caring for your land by allowing it to erode or by not applying good farming practices, and the like. You can even sin against the environment by disobeying man's laws designed to protect it, even by something as mundane but as pervasive as tossing trash out the window of your car. In such instances, the sin is one of pride (actually the root of all sin), in which one ignores the needs of other people for their own selfish short-term gain. For example, someone must eventually stoop over (humble themselves) to pick up that soft drink can you just tossed out the car window so, deep down, you must think you're better than that person, which definitively amounts to sin.

But no sinful offenses against animals are listed in the Bible and this fact is not an accident. God never intended mankind to abuse animals or the environment, of course, because His mandate is that we be good stewards. But failure to mention these as prohibited in the numerous lists of sins must mean that traditional animal stewardship and utilization, as it has been practiced down through the centuries, and traditional uses of the land, are well within the parameters of God's will. If abuse of animals or the environment occurred, it wasn't such a serious problem that God put a significant priority on it. Certainly it wasn't enough of a factor that it is included in any of these lists. If using animals in traditional fashion is a sin in any way, surely it would have shown up on one of these prominent records. The higher calling by far is obviously the command to love your fellow human beings. It is a perversion of major proportions if one loves animals (any animal) more than other people, and this applies even to the lowliest person (Romans 12:16). Only the sin of pride produces this kind of twisted thinking, a point also made by this same scriptural reference.

By now you surely get my drift. God's concern for animals pales very nearly to insignificance in comparison to His concern for His image-bearer. Animal rights activists will dispute this, but their position is fatally flawed. That will become even more apparent in the following chapters.

NOTES

1 www.jiva.org/vegetarian_athletes.htm, [accessed May 2008; no longer online]. Also www.veganfitness.net/forum/viewtopic.php, [accessed February 2009].

2 *The New York Times*, "Variety in Food," Sept. 12, 1880.

3 www.chetday.com/vegandietdangers.htm, [accessed February 2009].

4 *The British Journal of Psychiatry*, "Physical Complications in Anorexia Nervosa," Dec. 1988:153: 72-75.

5 J. Balint, *Pediatric Clinics of North America*, "Physical Findings in Nutritional Deficiency," Vol. 45, Issue 1, 245-260.

6 D. Milea, et al, "Blindness in a Strict Vegan," *New England Journal of Medicine*, 342:897, March 23, 2000, *Correspondence*.

7 Everett Harrison, *The Wycliffe Bible Commentary*, 1222.

8 John Walvoord and Roy Zuck, *The Bible Knowledge Commentary* (New Testament), Victor Books, Second printing, 1983, 492.

9 www.naiaonline.org/body/articles/archives/arterror.htm, National Animal Interest Alliance list, [accessed February 2009].

10 Southern Poverty Law Center, "From Push to Shove," *Intelligence Report*, Fall 2002, www.splc.org/intel/intelreport/article.jsp?aid=42, [accessed February 2009].

11 www.sover.net/~lsudlow/ARvsAW.htm, [accessed May 2009].

12 www.naiaonline.org.body/articles/archived_articles_extremism.htm, [accessed February 2009].

TEN

THE VEGETARIAN ANGLE

THE vegetarian lifestyle is widely and enthusiastically promoted as healthful, more compassionate, and better for the environment. While a case can be made that some aspect of each of these may hold a grain of truth, when taken as a whole this movement and its agenda don't add up. Let's start with a Biblical reference and build from there.

In Romans 1:18-25, it states, "For the wrath of God is revealed from heaven against all ungodliness and unrighteousness of men, who suppress the truth in unrighteousness, because that which is known about God is evident within them; for God made it evident to them. For since the creation of the world His invisible attributes, His eternal power and divine nature, have been clearly seen, being understood through *what had been made* [italics mine], so that they are without excuse. For even though they knew God, they did not honor Him as God, or give thanks; but they became futile in their speculations, and their foolish heart was darkened. Professing to be wise, they became fools, and exchanged the glory of the incorruptible God for an image in the form of corruptible man and of birds and four-footed animals and crawling creatures. Therefore, God gave them over in the lusts of their hearts to impurity, that their bodies might be dishonored among them. For they exchanged the truth of God for a lie, and worshiped and served the creature rather than the Creator, who is blessed forever."

There are a number of ideas in this passage that I want to inspect. Let's set some general principles that I believe are true.

Untruth Prevails Today

Animal rights proponents seem to revel in untruth.[1,2] Everything they push, apart from reasonable and humane treatment of animals, is a lie. Placing a value on animals that equals or surpasses the value God has unmistakably placed on His image-bearer is clearly sin, an obvious rebellion against God and His revealed Word (see again Jesus Christ's answer to the question as to the greatest commandment, found in Matthew 22:37-40). As we will discuss further below, even the diet they recommend is deadly, and "causes their bodies to be dishonored" by being poorly nourished and subject to numerous unnecessary diseases. Their so-called wisdom grows out of the false concept of godless evolution and man's supposed animal nature, and ties the animal rights movement firmly to the world's counterfeit values and ideas. If ever a philosophy were based on the twin pillars of speculation and phony science, it is this one.

Denying God's existence or claiming not to know about Him is no excuse for such a viewpoint (a main thrust of the Romans 1 passage quoted above). We will all be held accountable for how we spend this life God has given us. Many vegetarians apparently believe in the Hindu concept of reincarnation, or being given multiple additional chances at finding truth, which is a bogus concept if one believes the Bible because it clearly states, "it is appointed for men to die once and after that comes judgment." (Hebrews 9:27). The fact is that God is real and He is not silent, if one has ears to hear. He generally speaks to mankind today through what He has already said (the Holy Scriptures). Even apart from these, though, it is impossible to miss the vast body of evidence for God's existence and His activity, because these surround us in His creation every moment of every day. We are responsible for our reaction to what He has already made abundantly clear about Himself. When we take a step of faith and ask Him to reveal more of Himself, I know from experience that we will not be disappointed.

The militant vegetarian (vegan) movement is a natural, expected outgrowth of the animal rights movement. This lifestyle, which is advertised passionately as the key to healthy living is, instead, promotion of the anti-human concept of animal rights to the *detriment* of human health. In reality, this philosophy has nothing at all to do with either animal rights or animal welfare, nor with human health. Animal rights groups are astoundingly effective fund-raising machines and their activities generate huge volumes of contributions. They have the attention and sympathy of most media outlets because they are "kind" to animals, and they effectively disguise their real agenda. Their top officers make liberal incomes and benefits while most often generating little or no help at all for animals.

For example, the Humane Society of the United States (HSUS) is the biggest of all animal rights groups. A nonprofit Goliath, HSUS runs no animal shelters at all, yet 1995 figures show its president at the time, Paul Irwin, was paid $237,831 in salary, and its CEO, John Hoyt, was paid $209,051; in addition, both were paid "tens of thousands of dollars in bonuses."[1, 3] These figures would be at least twice as high in 2009 dollars. Furthermore, figures show that HSUS took in some $100 million in 2007, a figure that has become the norm in recent years. HSUS's chief executive and president, Wayne Pacelle, was paid $234,753 in salary and retirement benefits that year. In fact, five employees make more than $200,000 per year. Quite a few more make between $150,000 and $200,000 per year, and even a secretary and two assistant treasurers make more than $100,000 per year! More interesting facts about this frontline animal rights group include that it spends almost $3.5 million dollars a year on lobbying and owns automobiles worth more than $1 million. HSUS also lists almost $250 million in assets and, again, receives more than $100 million in annual income, most of it through direct contributions. Out of this massive war chest, HSUS allocates only a little more than $6 million in grants to like-minded groups and individuals, with little apparent oversight of how even that small fraction of their annual income is spent.[4] Many of the references I've cited in this section claim HSUS is much worse than I've portrayed them, contributing only 1.5 percent of its revenues to local animal shelters, while clinging to terrorist connections similar to the one described in a PETA case below.

Many watchdog groups allege that this nonprofit corporation spends practically everything it takes in on fundraising in one form or another, often hidden as "program expenses"—more than $75 million on its 2007 Form 990 referenced above—making it practically impossible to track where the money actually went.[1] One must suspect that many, if not most, salaried employees are involved in one way or another in fundraising, since that appears to be a vital function of the organization. Salaries would not show up under "fundraising." Even apart from this obvious possibility, *Worth* magazine recently gave HSUS a D rating for spending an inordinate amount on fundraising, and this same source rates HSUS among the worst-managed USA charities.[4] They and others[5, 6] have calculated that some 53 percent of its income is spent on more fundraising. Obviously by design, HSUS does not break down its expenditures in a way that allows one to see the extent of its disconnection from the real world, and it performs little or no frontline work to actually promote animal welfare. In reality, HSUS runs no animal shelters or adoption services,[1, 4] although it contributes to some animal shelters through grants to various subsidiary organizations. Online rating sites note that even the *admitted* direct fundraising costs at HSUS are nearly triple those of other charities of comparable size, such as Samaritan's Purse. The huge HSUS corporate family reportedly has no active governing board overseeing its overall structure, among other shortcomings.[3, 4] A list of unpaid board members is included on its Form 990, but whether these people have the authority to make decisions and enforce them within the organization is unclear.

It cannot be overemphasized that charity watchdog groups have a very low opinion of this mega-animal rights group. If you have doubts, spend some time online reading what unbiased ratings organizations (see references 1-6) have to say about HSUS.

Another meatless group with a high income and a suspicious record of supporting domestic terrorism is one we have already discussed, namely the organization People for the Ethical Treatment of Animals (PETA).[2, 7, 8] This activist organization has annual contributions that exceed $30 million, according to its website (www.peta.org), but does not post its Form 990 online so it can be publicly scrutinized. However, this form is available from PETA for a small fee, so I ordered it. Even apart from its Form

990, the official figures given on its website show admitted fundraising activity to be at least double the norm, and it is impossible to tell whether massive additional fundraising expenses are hidden under its 83.5 percent "program expenses."

Even examination of PETA's Form 990 leaves many of these questions unanswered. Out of $33 million received in income in 2007, admitted direct fundraising accounted for about 12 percent of income, about twice that of Samaritan's Purse. Under a section titled Program Services Accomplishments, more than $8 million is listed for publications distribution to "students, teachers, the general public, and supporters." One would wonder if all these publications were completely devoid of fundraising aspects. Another item on the "accomplishments" list is nearly $9 million for high-profile persecution of various businesses that use animals in some way. These actions generate publicity that likely evokes contributions from supporters, so they might also be categorized as "fundraising," in my opinion. Exactly $4,413,923 was distributed to a plethora of organizations, all with the stated purpose to "support program activities," whatever that means. No further elaboration is given.

PETA is far bolder in its activism than even HSUS. Quoting one respected source: "Earlier this week, PETA called for U.S. networks to stop televising the Westminster Dog Show, citing the BBC film as evidence of unacceptable deformity and disease in pedigree dogs. *Pedigree Dogs Exposed* was the result of two years' careful research. The film highlighted serious health and welfare concerns in pedigree dogs that many experts agree need to be addressed urgently. However, the filmmakers have no connection to PETA and are ideologically opposed to PETA's aims. 'I am horrified that PETA is using our film to further its own, warped agenda,' says Jemima Harrison of Passionate Productions, which made the film for the BBC. 'Our film is about animal welfare, not animal rights. PETA's animal-welfare record is appalling. It kills 97 percent of the dogs that come to its shelters and admits its ultimate aim is to rid the world of what it calls the 'domestic enslavement' of dogs as either pets or working dogs. In stark contrast, and the reason we made the film, is that we believe pedigree dogs are of tremendous value to society and that something needs to be done to arrest the damage caused by decades of inbreeding and selection for beauty. The film is a passionate call for urgent reform to save them before it is too late. To do that, there needs to be urgent reform of breeding practices and dog shows. PETA is a bunch of crackpots who do not care about anything but publicity and making money. They have not bothered to contact us, and, indeed, if they did, we would make it very clear we do not want their support. It devalues and marginalizes a film that raises a serious issue that needs to be addressed, and quickly."[9]

This group also has been roundly and appropriately criticized for supporting animal rights terrorism. For example, the following quote: "In 1992, animal rights activist and Earth Liberation Front member Rod Coronado was convicted and sentenced to four years in federal prison for setting fire to a research laboratory at Michigan State University, causing more than $2.5 million in damage. Coronado's defense fund was supplemented by a $45,000 donation by PETA as well as an additional $25,000 'loan' to Coronado's father, who later admitted that the loan was, in fact, not a loan at all. When questioned about the money given to Coronado, PETA President Ingrid Newkirk told ABC's John Stossel that Coronado was entitled to a legal defense, and that he was a 'fine young man, and a schoolteacher.' Newkirk and PETA said nothing to condemn the arson."[10]

According to this same source, which used PETA tax records to compile much of its data, the FBI has labeled both Animal Liberation Front (ALF) and Earth Liberation Front (ELF) as domestic terror groups.[10] The FBI is quoted as saying that in the last ten years, it is believed that ALF and ELF have committed more than six hundred criminal acts with damages of more than $43 million. John Lewis, the FBI's deputy assistant director for counterterrorism, said animal and environmental rights extremists have claimed credit for more than 1,200 criminal incidents since 1990. The FBI has 150 pending investigations associated with animal rights or eco-terrorist activities, and ATF officials say they have opened 58 investigations in the past six years related to violence attributed to ELF and ALF. Both groups appear to have unwavering support from their presumed parent organization and staunch supporter, PETA.

Misdirected endeavors of the animal rights movement lead to much animal (as well as human) suffering, not animal welfare. But practically all organizations under this dubious banner apparently don't care so long as the contributions come in. Raising money is the bottom line, and they will embrace any cause, no matter how destructive it is to an animal or a population of animals, if there is money to be raised. This has been demonstrated time and again in the animal rights movement.

I must say again that promotion of the vegetarian lifestyle is *not* designed to improve the lot of animals and it is emphatically *not* a way to improved human health. Indeed, I believe it is a sign of predicted tribulation fanaticism that will give rise to a murderous antichrist, also named in the Bible as "the Beast," according to premillennial theology.

Scientists: Zero Meat Is Unhealthy

There is nothing inherently wrong with being a sensible vegetarian, but radical vegetarians (who generally are those most heavily into animal rights) drastically downplay the significant health risks of this lifestyle. A wise vegetarian realizes the limitations they face and the need for supplementation with moderate amounts of animal products to achieve a healthy balance in their diet. I have read statements by vegans who claim that it is unfair to point out that they *must* get vitamin B12 from an animal source since everyone ultimately gets it from bacteria or yeast, but it is a point that has to be made and emphasized repeatedly until the majority of people know about it. This vitamin is always produced by certain microorganisms, even when it is obtained in the normal fashion by the needy individual—from meat, where animals store it in high quantities. As for yeast and bacteria, few would deny that these tiny creatures are but minute animals whose complex genetic programs allow them to manufacture the intricate molecule cyanocobalamin—also known as vitamin B12—which is essential to life.

I am not being picky in pointing this out; I am simply clarifying the untenable position that strict vegetarians must defend if they are steeped in animal rights philosophy. Rather than taking extreme measures to avert the death of animals (or their reasonable use to provide dairy products or eggs), it would be infinitely more honest to admit the unavoidable need and do what is most sensible. Not only do animal products provide crucial vitamin B12, they also handily provide all the amino acids and minerals that are difficult (and in some cases practically impossible) to obtain from plants. One needn't eat meat in order to live, because God has provided these secondary products for those who choose a no-meat lifestyle. Only if one is promoting a radical animal rights agenda does one need to avoid eggs and dairy products.

Here is one misleading statement, credited to Dr. Dean Ornish of CNN's WebMD, which fits perfectly the definition in the passage from Romans above: "When you eat a lot of meat, it takes a long time for it to make its way through your digestive tract. As it putrefies and decays, your breath smells bad, your sweat smells bad, and your bowels smell bad—not very attractive. You may want to lose weight to attract people to you, but when they get too close, it becomes counterproductive. Eating a lot of meat instead of all those simple carbohydrates will help lower their insulin response, causing them to lose weight. But they're mortgaging their health in the process." [11]

Very nearly every idea in this quote can be effectively and legitimately challenged. A high-protein, low-carbohydrate diet is easily processed by the human body, because when God gave positive instructions for man to eat meat (Genesis 9:3), He had already provided for its easy digestibility. Almost certainly the necessary stomach acids and other digestive elements for processing meat efficiently were there all along, but lay dormant until they were needed. For example, hydrochloric acid is needed to digest protein, and it isn't found in the stomach of herbivorous animals, but is plentiful in man. Likewise, the pancreas has all the necessary complicated enzymes to digest meat, something that can't be said of a sheep or cow. In fact, a quality study has clearly shown that the human digestive tract is far more similar to that of a dog (a carnivore) than to that of a sheep (a herbivore). [12, 13]

Certainly you can fill the stomach with so much food of any kind that it takes time to clear, but meat in moderation rather easily digests and provides wonderfully for every possible need of the human body. It never rots or decays in the human intestinal tract, because the body efficiently puts it to work far too rapidly for that to occur. [14, 15] It is quickly broken down into its component essential amino acids, glucose, and other important nutrients, and thus is put to work right away. It has been known for almost a century that meat stimulates good digestion, in fact, far better than a vegetarian diet.[16]

Eskimos for centuries (perhaps millennia) ate a diet as near to purely meat as one can get. They enjoyed excellent health, while early Arctic explorers died of scurvy due to a deficiency of vitamin C, which is found richly in animal fats, especially seal blubber. I have visited more than a dozen Inuit, Inuvialuit, and Inupiat communities in the Arctic of Canada and Alaska, and I have seldom seen an overweight or diabetic individual in those societies. The traditional all-meat Inuit diet, uncomplicated by encroachment of foods and habits from the temperate zones, has been shown to be highly effective at preventing heart disease.[17] This is changing, however, as aspects of the white man's diet have become much more common there than in former times, and, unfortunately, a high percentage of adult Arctic natives smoke cigarettes (this is my personal observation).

It was demonstrated decades ago that bowel gases hardly exist in people on a pure meat diet.[18] Gas is produced by digestion of complex carbohydrates (which are those not extensively refined, as are white sugar and fine flour), and not by meat. Even if you are not a vegetarian, try Dr. Ornish's diet[19] for a short time and see how much foul gas you begin producing, and it doesn't take very long for it to start happening. Don't overdo your trial run, though, because your risk of heart disease and stroke goes up dramatically on his diet, since it causes the ratio of total cholesterol to HDL cholesterol (the good kind) to move in the wrong direction. Moreover, the risk of cardiovascular disease, as well as breast and colon cancer, was found to be statistically unaffected by eating such an unnecessarily low-fat diet.[20]

These allegations are not my own, either; they are supported by the American Medical Association, the American Heart Association, the American Diabetic Association, and the American Stroke Association, none of which recommends a strict vegetarian diet, a very telling piece of information. These groups (and virtually all mainline medical associations) are quite obviously interested in human health and not in promoting a false religion.

In fact, a diet high in carbohydrates and nearly devoid of fat leads to numerous serious diseases that a simple slice of red meat weekly would improve or cure completely. Skin diseases are particularly prominent among strict vegetarians, as are inflammatory bowel disease, sexual dysfunction in both men and women, heart disease, cancer, and stroke, probably due to deficiency of omega-3 fatty acids found most richly in cold-water fish. Some of the shortest-lived people on earth are strict vegetarians, such as those who live in southern India. To quote: "The vegetarians of southern India eat a low-calorie diet very high in carbohydrates and low in protein and fat. They have the shortest life span of any society on Earth, and their bodies have an extremely low muscle mass. They are weak and frail and the children clearly exhibit a failure to thrive. Their heart-disease rate is double that of the meat eaters in northern India."[21]

This is certainly not an accident, and it isn't revealed by proponents of this unhealthy lifestyle in any of their literature. Indications are[22,23,24] that many of the vocal advocates of the drastic vegan diet are afflicted with these diseases, though they hide it well from the general public and from their suffering followers. Some call this unhealthy obsession with avoiding animal products a mental disease or an eating disorder, which no doubt it can be in some cases. I might not make a general statement so broad, because it is easily controllable by an individual's daily choices. However, certainly such a way of life has every characteristic of a false religion, including many deceived and committed followers.

By contrast, numerous studies have indicated that meat-eating peoples live longer, healthier lives. The Russian Caucasus region, where I have hunted several times and where I am again hunting even now as I review this material, is home to some of the longest-living humans on earth, and they subsist on a diet high in pork fat and other animal products.[25] In fact, I helped my hosts harvest and butcher three yaks for winter meat just yesterday. On one foray to hunt high-mountain game in the Caucasus a couple of years ago, we had not only sausages and cheese as staples, but also took along live chickens (which we humorously named Wednesday, Thursday, Friday, etc). They fed and foraged obliviously about the camp until it was their day to give their all.

The people of the Hunza Valley of the Himalayas (where India,

Pakistan, and China converge—another place I have visited while hunting) are actually longer-lived than people of the Caucasus Mountains. Some vegetarian activists have stated that these Himalayan people are vegetarians, but I know from personal observation that this isn't true. The Hunza people include in their diet generous portions of dairy products and adequate amounts of meat.[26, 27]

Meatless Diet Equals Population Control

One well-publicized case of child abuse landed both vegan parents in jail when their daughter was found to be severely malnourished for lack of animal products (or even breast milk). The child weighed only 10 pounds at age 15 months, had no teeth, her abdomen was swollen, and she could neither talk nor sit up. Her abuse began at conception, and her delayed development was certainly due to a rampaging deficiency of nutrient-rich animal products that are easily obtained and quickly digested.[28]

Another similar case resulted in the death of a six-week-old infant whose vegan parents fed him a diet of soy milk and apple juice. The baby weighed only three and a half pounds when it died. Both parents were sentenced to life in prison for murder.[29] Even a cursory search of the internet reveals that this kind of tragedy is all too common among adherents to the radical vegan lifestyle.

The Romans 1 passage I quoted at the beginning of this section is central to understanding the vegetarian push by extremists. Like their close kin, the radical environmentalists, these fanatics usually are convinced that there are too many people in the world and that the human population must be reduced by every available means. Myriad internet sites are dedicated to reducing the human population by 90 percent or more by whatever method it takes to accomplish this—genocide by policy, one might say.

Pushing an unhealthy diet as the secret to long life and prosperity is one way to achieve the "ideal" goal of less than a half-billion people on the planet. Billionaire Ted Turner has stated the real goal of the extremist environmental movement very clearly: "Global climate change…is caused by too many people…. We need to 'stabilize' the population."[30] This is in perfect alignment with the radical agenda of the extremist environmental movement, and is another immutable tie between this camp and the animal rights movement. Actually, according to Sheldon Richman, the entire population of the earth today could fit into the state of Texas, allowing each individual 1,000 square feet of living space, demonstrating that ours isn't a problem of population but of distribution. He also points out that every human being on the planet could fit into Jacksonville, Florida, with adequate standing room.[31] Moreover, an article in the *New York Times* affirms that there exist some 300 pounds of insect for every pound of human being on the planet, representing ten quintillion bugs (10^{18}, or 10 followed by 18 zeros, or 10 billion billion)[32] at any given time. And humans are responsible for global warming?

As I mentioned above, this viewpoint taken as a whole is actually a false religion, because all parties refuse to see the Creator God when they look upon "what has been made." Instead, they effectively "worship and serve the creature rather than the Creator." This would include revering some humans, especially those at the top of the hierarchy who are famous or who formulate effective propaganda, plus "four-footed animals, birds, and crawling creatures." In so doing they commit a grave error and miss the fact that they are seeking to diminish both God's status and the status of His image-bearer. This whole philosophy is predicted in the Bible, and we will shortly cover how this epidemic in the future will reach devastating and genocidal proportions. Though this destruction appears to me to be inevitable during the coming reign of the Beast, I would be remiss not to share what God has revealed to me with anyone who will listen.

The following chapter is dedicated to the connection between the modern radical-environmental and animal rights movements. Please allow me to emphasize again that environmental extremism is undeniably well-connected to the vegetarian and animal rights movements. All these groups claim that keeping livestock is inefficient, wastes resources that could be dedicated to vegetarian interests, and contributes to pollution. All of these fail to recognize the fact that two-thirds of the earth's surface is too dry or mountainous for utilization as cropland, yet animals efficiently transform otherwise inedible vegetation found there into excellent protein and other nutrients suitable for human beings. The argument is practically irrefutable that converting the whole world to vegetarianism would lead to massive human starvation.[33, 34] Sadly, I believe that this awful scenario may be played out to the fullest under the final Antichrist.

A Tool of Satan

Another important passage of Scripture I cannot fail to mention is 1 Timothy 4:1-5, which states "But the Spirit [God's Holy Spirit—brackets mine] explicitly says that in later times some will fall away from the faith, paying attention to deceitful spirits and doctrines of demons, by means of the hypocrisy of liars…men who forbid marriage and who *advocate abstaining from certain foods* [italics mine] which God has created to be gratefully shared in by those who believe and know the truth." These "certain foods" would clearly consist entirely of meat, as today's experience with the animal rights movement confirms. This is a very serious charge against those who are committed to avoiding all meat, because it unambiguously reveals their unseen motivation. Though his ultimate defeat was assured by the victory of Christ through the cross and the resurrection, Satan is alive and well in the world today, and part of his program is to promote unhealthy lifestyles. He apparently functions under certain God-imposed constraints (2 Thessalonians 2:7), but still he has an agenda. He uses human agents to accomplish many parts of that agenda, which is to deceive the whole of mankind and promote his own lies as wise and truthful. Jesus Christ called him "a liar and the father of lies" (John 8:44). We are seeing this prediction, the preaching of the no-meat lifestyle, fulfilled vividly today in the animal rights movement and its vegetarian-advocacy program.

Am I saying the animal rights movement is of Satan and that it is directed by demons? I don't know, but it certainly appears to me that it is! How else could it be promoting an unhealthy lifestyle for human beings in the name of "animal rights"? How else could its more violent adherents commit murder and mayhem among their innocent brothers and sisters (fellow bearers of the image of God, whom they should love instead of murdering)? These fellow image-bearers happen to make their living or have their enjoyment in a way God has ordained and sanctioned, i.e., through animal utilization. How else could animal rights fanatics care not the least if innumerable animals die because of their activities, revealing that they have no interest in animal welfare, while at the same time clinging to a morbid interest in animal rights orthodoxy? If you so much as own a pet, you are in their sights for destruction as much as the person who hunts deer or elk, or the scientist who does medical research using mice. They may be concentrating elsewhere for the moment, but you are on their schedule.

Please take special note of the following statements. In saying these things, I am by no means alleging that every *individual* with an animal rights outlook is under demonic control. Many are simply naïve or deceived and, hopefully, by reading the material in this book and doing their own personal search for the truth, they can "come to their senses and escape the snare of the devil" (2 Timothy 2:26). One statement I think is unequivocal, however: If you are a radical animal rights proponent, you *cannot* also be a Christian in close fellowship with your Creator through an *agape* love relationship to His sacrificed Son, Jesus Christ; or you are severely misguided. Butchers, medical researchers, cattle and hog farmers, hunters, and others who utilize animals *can* and *do* often enjoy this godly eternal relationship, but the radical animal rights proponent could be excluded by his rebellion against God and His revealed Word. The only way salvation can come to them (or to anyone) is through a repentant heart and submission to the authority of the Word of God.

I firmly believe that Satan is busily using poor, defrauded people to prepare for his limited day of absolute power on earth. The forces of righteousness, those people indwelt by God's Holy Spirit, will win in the end when Jesus Christ returns, but much death and destruction are predicted before that time. Meanwhile, Satan needs as many ways as he can find to exercise absolute control over a terrified human population. As Jesus Christ said many times, "He who has ears, let him hear" (Matthew 11:15; Mark 4:9; Luke 8:8).

I hope I've convinced you that a vegetarian diet is not the best or healthiest diet. I assure you, it isn't. It can't even possibly taste the best. My wife Linda and I follow a healthful weekly plan: Deer meat, 4-5 ounces twice a week (killed by me with a single shot to the animal's head, the deer then gutted and drained of blood within five minutes of the shot, then hung in a cooler for 5-7 days at 39° Fahrenheit to "age" and become more tender, after which we personally cut and wrap it—Linda and I eat about four animals per year so prepared); fresh or fresh-frozen salmon or halibut on one or two other days (any fresh fish will do, but these two kinds are especially rich in heart-healthy omega-3 fatty acids—and they give us an excuse to go fishing!); chicken or turkey one or two days a week, and pork or lamb on another day. (Ah, all these are a "soothing aroma" to—well, to me, and to the Lord as well! See Exodus 29:18, 25). Linda's accompaniments: Fresh or fresh-frozen garden vegetables, two or three kinds in generous portions baked lightly in olive oil, a mixed salad or raw carrots, celery, or other crunchies on the side. Those veggies grown in our garden are best, but good quality grocery-store vegetables are fine, too. I don't care what kind of commercial fertilizer we use, so long as it replenishes the soil, because it all comes out the same in the plant. We have no mercy on any insects that attack, using the most effective modern chemical controls available—just wash or peel your harvest before you eat it. I do use non-commercial fertilizers such as manure, too, and I have nothing against going completely organic in a garden, either, if you want, but it's not for me. If organic is your thing, just be sure to cut away the bug bites and don't eat any worms along with your vegetables, unless you need the extra vitamin B12. Add to this fare whole-grain bread, one slice; and fruit, yogurt, ice cream, or sherbet for dessert.

I've been eating this kind of food for years, and I recently hunted mountain game with 27 Sherpa guides in Nepal at 15,000 feet at the age of 63, and right now I'm on an airliner from Tajikistan, where I hunted mountain sheep in some of the roughest terrain imaginable (I am now 64). I challenge you to accompany me on such a hunt, whether you're a vegetarian or not. If you do happen to be a strict vegan, odds are high that you can't do it at all.

If you're interested in a truly healthful and scrumptious diet, check out a few of Linda's recipes in the Appendix at the end of this book. You can buy "wild" game meat in many specialty stores, though it is domesticated and obviously not as good as that which the hunter kills in the wild and prepares himself from A to Z. Not everyone can be a hunter, though, so it's a good substitute.

NOTES

1 www.activistcash.com/organization_overview.cfm?oid=136, [accessed March 2009].

2 www.sover.net/~lsudlow/ARvsAW.htm, [accessed May 2009].

3 www.charitynavigator.org; Humane Society of the United States, Form 990 posted on its website (www.hsus.org) (also filed with the Internal Revenue Service).

4 www.give.org, now under America's Better Business Bureau [accessed May 2008].

5 www.consumerfreedom.com/news_detail.cfm/headline/3899 [accessed May 2009].

6 www.activistcash.com/organization_blackeye.cfm/oid/136 [accessed May 2009].

7 Spencer Hsu, "FBI Papers Show Terror Inquiries into PETA, Other Groups Tracked," *The Washington Post*, Dec. 20, 2005.

8 www.frontrowfreakshow.blogspot.com/2005/04/eat-peta.html [accessed February 2009].

9 www.dogmagazine.net/archives/1668/pedigree-dogs-exposed-film-maker-hits-out-at-animal-rights-extremists, Jan. 8, 2009 [accessed February 2009].

10 Terry Frieden, "BFI, ATF Address Domestic Terrorism," CNN, May 19, 2005.

11 www.webmd.com/content/pages/1/3080_360.htm [accessed May 2008—apparently this quote has been removed as it is no longer available, though an interview with Dr. Ornish outlining many details of his "heart-healthy" diet is on the site as of Feb. 2009]; quote still online at www.biblelife.org/animal_rights.htm.

12 W. L. Voegtlin, *The Stone Age Diet*, Vantage Press, Inc., NY (1975), 44-45.

13 http://paleodiet.com/comparison.html [accessed May 2009].

14 D. Remond, et al, "Postprandial Whole-Body Protein Metabolism after a Meat Meal…," *American Journal of Clinical Nutrition*, 85:1286-1292, 2007.

15 www.tuberose.com/Digestion.html, [accessed February 2009].

16 M. Rehfus and G. Marcil, "Meat for Digestion," *Time* magazine, April 8, 1929.

17 Centre Hospitalier Universitaire de Quebec, Laval University, and University of Geulph, "Traditional Inuit Diet Cuts Heart Disease Risk," *American Journal of Clinical Nutrition*, October 2001.

18 Vilhjalmur Stefansson, "Eskimos Prove All-Meat Diet Provides Excellent Health," *Harper's Monthly,* Nov. 1935.

19 Dean Ornish, www.webmd.com/diet/ornish-diet-what-it-is, [accessed Feb. 2009].

20 Ross L. Prentice, PH.D., et al, "Eight Year Study Finds Small Risk Reduction from Lower Dietary Fat," *Journal of the American Medical Association,* Feb. 2006.

21 H. L. Abrams, Jr., "Vegetarianism: An Anthropological/Nutritional Evaluation," *Journal of Applied Nutrition,* 1980, 32:2:53-87.

22 Joel Furhman, "Leaders in the Vegan Movement Develop Parkinson's: Case Studies," April 15, 2009; "What Vegans May Be Missing," May 22, 2009, www.diseaseproof.com/archives/healthy-food-leaders-of-the-vegan-movement-develop-parkinson's-case-studies.html, [accessed May 2009].

23 Nina Planck, "Death by Veganism," *The New York Times,* May 21, 2007.

24 Mark Sisson, "My Escape from Vegan Island," Mark's Daily Apple, www.marksdailyapple.com/vegan-island/, [accessed May 2009].

25 Thomas Moore, *Lifespan: What Really Affects Human Longevity?* Simon & Schuster, NY (1990).

26 John Clark, *Hunza: Lost Kingdom of the Himalayas,* Funk and Wagnells (1956).

27 S. Fallon and M. Enig, *Nourishing Traditions,* Chapter 5, New Trends Publishing; Washington, D.C. (2000).

28 www.hugesettlements.com/Personal-Injury/3098.html, [accessed Feb. 2009].

29 *The Atlanta Journal-Constituion,* "Vegan Couple Sentenced to Life in Prison," May 9, 2007.

30 www.LifeSiteNews.com, April 8, 2008: "Turner's Depopulation Plan" [accessed February 2009].

31 Sheldon Richman, Senior Fellow and Editor, The Future of Freedom Foundation; Editor, *The Freeman*; Senior Editor, Cato Institute, on CNN, Oct. 5, 2007, and at www.cato.org/testimony/ct-ps720.html, [accessed February 2009].

32 Natalie Angier, "What's Creepy, Crawly, and Big in Movies? Bugs," *The New York Times,* Feb. 18, 1991.

33 Public Broadcasting System, *The Charlie Rose Show,* April 1, 2008.

34 www.ansi.okstate.edu/breeds, Breeds of Livestock, Oklahoma State University, Department of Animal Science.

ELEVEN

THE KEY CONNECTION: THE SPIRIT OF ANTICHRIST AND MODERN ENVIRONMENTALISM

An Immutable Partnership

As you may have noted in the previous chapter, it is impossible to write about the animal rights movement without bringing more into focus their chief allies—today's radical environmental movement. There is a strong connection between animal rights proponents and hype over the benefits of a vegetarian lifestyle, as well as a firm connection between both lifestyles and the earth-worshipping heresy. The environmental and animal rights movements work in concert, at least on the surface. Both pressure groups are out to "save the planet" in their own way, and both are predicted in the Bible as agents of the ultimate Antichrist. Here I will try to make the essential association between them, because it is critical to understanding their methods and motivations.

Let me say first of all that the issue of fundraising is not a small one. Both factions practice effective deception of both the government and their public supporters so they maintain tax-exempt status and receive the maximum amount in contributions as well as massive government grants. These organizations are out to destroy the very fabric of our society in slightly different ways, yet they do so with the blessing of our own government and generous access to taxpayer money! Each has officers, by and large, who live luxuriously, receive liberal salaries, and no doubt consider themselves among the elite. Both groups conduct effective fund-raising events and jealously guard their territories. Normally they work together well, but they maintain an appropriate separation that maximizes contributions to both animal rights and environmental concerns. A person interested in memorializing their poodle with a multi-million dollar contribution may have a far different set of priorities from a person who sees the oil companies as the epitome of evil, or humanity as the chief enemy of the environment. Still, there is great overlap in the positions of these two camps. Both are legendary in their ability to raise funds from an unsuspecting general population that will eventually become their victims, a tragedy I outline more fully in Chapter Twelve.

The first Bible reference to which I would point is 1 Thessalonians 5:2-3, which states, "For you yourselves know full well that the day of the Lord will come just like a thief in the night. While they are saying, 'Peace and safety!' then destruction will come upon them suddenly like labor pains upon a woman with child; and they shall not escape."

This would include people in general, of course, but radical environmentalists are the obvious standard-bearers, since they are in the forefront of alarmist propaganda designed to scare people into following their hysterical agenda. People will become so fearful of much-touted impending environmental catastrophes that they may accept any leader who promises to deliver them from these kinds of dangers. They may even welcome any kind of world government that promises "peace and safety," but the Word of God is clear that there is no security apart from God Himself.

Government Complicity

This mindset is an everyday headline, so little elaboration is necessary. Every American has been touched in some way by these movements, at the very least by wasted tax money to defend against their lawsuits. Global warming—now being cleverly renamed as "climate change" or "climate chaos"—is the current battle cry, as the environment, endangered species, air pollution, marine mammals, spotted owls, snail darters, kangaroo rats, wetlands, and the like have been in the past.

The "day of the Lord" is predicted in numerous Old Testament passages (Joel 2:1, 11; Zephaniah 1:14-18). It will be a terrible day for unbelievers, a fact that is underscored in the New Testament. (Matthew 24:29-44; Hebrews 12:26-27; 1 Thessalonians 4:16-17, Revelation 6:14-17; 19:11-16).It will be a time that comes after a radical apparent savior of mankind arises, empowered by Satan, to deceive the whole human race into believing he is sent from God. In actuality he will be an agent of Satan, the central part of an unholy trinity that includes Satan, the Beast (the Antichrist), and the false prophet (the evil equivalent of John the Baptist). These three are understood as well by many to be the wicked counterparts of Father, Son, and Holy Spirit.

Conditioning the population of the United States to receive the Beast can be traced in part, I believe, to a piece of major legislation passed in 1973, when the Endangered Species Act (ESA) became law. This innocuous-sounding law has been an absolute bonanza for both environmental and animal rights activists, and a horrible disaster for the bountiful freedom that has historically characterized the American way of life. It has spawned money-gobbling bureaucracies that do practically nothing for the environment or endangered animals. It continues to be the focal point of innumerable lawsuits to the point that the U.S. Fish and Wildlife Service, which is charged with enforcing the law, making rules related to it, and defending lawsuits that arise out of their decisions, spends practically all its budget doing the latter.[1] A check of this reference will show that more than 90 percent of the lawsuits are filed and funded by radical environmental groups and animal rights groups such as Defenders of Wildlife and the Center for Biological Diversity. Very few are brought by animal utilization groups, which generally have ongoing, proven conservation projects that eat up most of their funds. From this information, one can easily deduce that these radical groups have little else on which to spend their money besides fundraising and lawsuits.

Following in the wake of the ESA came more environmental "dream laws," specifically the Marine Mammal Protection Act, the Wetlands Act, the Environmental Policy Act, the Clean Air Act, the Clean Water Act, almost ad infinitum. For the most part, all any of these has done is simply add to the war chest of radicals and cost the taxpayer huge amounts of money for little to no return on the investment.

Those who wrote and passed these laws could not foresee it at the time, but today few reasonable people would deny that all these acts have been used to halt human development in wholesale fashion. Still, no one in authority has the backbone or the power to challenge the environmental juggernaut. Some have tried, but no one has had the clout to push through the needed changes to these odious laws (the only really effective change would consist of their total repeal). It is sad to say so, but I believe there will be no relief from any of these, and that additional laws, even more dreadful and more threatening to our very survival as a nation, will be forthcoming shortly. This seems inevitable in view of Biblical prophecy, and there are actually quite a few such laws pending in various Congressional committees even as I write this. Individual freedom and private property rights in America are what are really endangered, and it becomes more so with passage of each new piece of legislation. The nation would truly be better served if Congress and the President would simply take a holiday for a few years, especially if they aren't going to repeal these anti-human, anti-progress laws. Needless to say, I have become regrettably cynical when it comes to supporting anyone aspiring to public office.

New roads are only one of many progressive projects these laws have stymied. Among other things, it has become practically impossible to build new electric power plants, and even difficult to build new schools and hospitals. Roads may the most visible point of obstructionism, however. In my own town, a bypass route was blocked for more than twenty years, mainly because every possible route traversed some obscure section of wetlands. The final route chosen is highly serpentine to avoid most low-lying areas, drastically increasing the cost and decreasing the road's efficiency and effectiveness.

Get this point unmistakably: If the United States had not already built our vast, essential interstate highway system, it would not be possible to construct it today because of lawsuits, obstructionism, and opposition that would arise over practically every mile, and all of it made possible only by this plethora of laws. While you're motoring along the interstate sometime, think of this. It would be impossible to build the road you're enjoying had construction begun after 1973. We should thank God that we were able to get this major project well on toward completion before the advent of these draconian measures.

It isn't just the radical environmentalists who are obstructing progress, either. The U.S. government has employed these and other odious laws to skyrocket regulation and interfere in new construction of all kinds, a phenomenon that spawns budgetary increases for various departments of these bureaucracies, adds government jobs, and boosts the salaries and power of top-echelon officials. These laws actually require the Federal government (and usually also the state government) to intervene in practically every construction project to make certain all provisions of numerous well-intended laws are followed. This requirement has spawned a vast jungle of paperwork, red tape, and formalities that will surely still be functioning when you and I are in our graves. Still, even when all governmental provisions are in order, environmentalist lawsuits are very nearly inevitable almost any time dirt is moved for any reason.[2,3] It doesn't matter how much it costs the country, or even how many environmental protections are included in such projects. In one major road project, 15 percent of the total cost, or some $370 million, was designated for environmental improvements along the route of the road. Despite this, the project was threatened with a new law that would have halted construction years after it began.[4]

Unhindered Global Competition

China and India have the most robust emerging economies in the world, and they labor under no such capricious restraints as I describe above. China is building coal-fired electric plants at the rate of one every few weeks, with 562 plants in some stage of development as this is written. India isn't too far behind, with 213 coal-fired electric plants in the construction phase.[5] Neither country is hampered by a significant environmental movement, so that even if the United States is shut down completely by animal rights and environmental activism, it will be only a minuscule contribution to reducing world carbon emissions. Europe is 80 percent nuclear, while we've been able to build precious few power plants in the USA, apart from those fueled by natural gas, since 1973. Our most plentiful resource is coal, and the USA has even been called

"The Saudi Arabia of coal." Despite this, only seven coal-fired plants are under construction in the USA, with 47 currently on the drawing boards.[5] Forty-seven percent of our current electric plants are fueled by plentiful coal, but only 19 percent of our power plants are nuclear.[7]

To build a new power plant approaches impossibility in the USA, due to the odious array of environmental laws and the legal actions that arise out of them, usually requiring years to satisfy or circumvent. Productive, legitimate jobs have been lost by the hundreds of thousands, and additional economic losses are staggering, yet any attempt to reform or reduce abuse of these laws is met by the stiffest resistance. The operative phrase, in response to even proposed minor revision of these detestable laws, is "gutting" the law in question. Were it up to most sensible people, we wouldn't only "gut" these obstructive pieces of ill-advised legislation, we'd slit their throats entirely and start over again, with an eye to preventing misuse of any new laws to stymie progress in our country.

To quote one source and reemphasize this point, "In a report compiled in early 2007, the U.S. Department of Energy listed 151 coal-fired power plants in the planning stages and talked about a resurgence in coal-fired electricity. But during 2007, 59 proposed U.S. coal-fired power plants were either refused licenses by state governments or quietly abandoned. In addition to the 59 plants that were dropped, close to 50 more coal plants are being contested in the courts, and the remaining plants will likely be challenged as they reach the permitting stage."[8] The laws being used to challenge these essential plants are the ones I list above, of course. My question is this: Where is our energy going to come from as we run out of oil and natural gas? Our only short-term option is coal. The radical environmentalist answer to this question is *very* simple, straightforward, and telling: "We don't care." And they truly don't. Apparently their vision for America is 100 million bison producing copious carbon dioxide on the plains instead of "amber waves of grain" making both food and oxygen, and a pristine forest with no people—other than an elite backpacking few, which includes them, of course—from coast to coast.[9]

The reason we are falling behind the rest of the world in numerous areas, and the reason our way of life is being directly threatened, is absolutely tied to this bevy of "dream laws." As emphasized, the whole lot should be repealed entirely and perhaps replaced with sensible, workable legislation that is pared down to only the bare essentials when it comes to government interference. However, a Congress and Administration with the vision, commitment, and fortitude to accomplish this will almost certainly never come to pass. It seems that Washington has completely lost the ability to "put America first" in its zeal to conform to the agenda of the omnipotent green movement. Because of this, it is absolutely inevitable that our beloved country is destined for eventual severe decline, perhaps to Third World status. The point is that these pieces of legislation were slipped past the American people disguised as something good for the nation, its people, and the environment, including wildlife; unfortunately, it turns out they are good only to promote a radical agenda that will unquestionably prepare the way for the apocalypse. That they are effective in this regard is hardly debatable.

Ahead: A Clear Road to Despair

The outcome of strict enforcement of these laws is easy to predict. What will occur over time is that the human race in the USA (and ultimately all over the world) will become so afraid of shortages, lawlessness, disease, famine, changing weather patterns, pollution, and innumerable other frightening events that fear will drive them to accept drastic measures to "save the planet." With intense governmental oversight and obstructionism at every level, it appears to me that our country may very well lead the way in developing this mind-set. Such adverse circumstances will be portrayed that people will accept anyone who demonstrates a capacity to lead. They will think that in such a person there is safety and redemption, but instead they will find wholesale destruction.

I believe this is a description of both the animal rights and radical environmental movements. Both appear to be environment-oriented, pro-stewardship, and wise; instead both are the acme of foolishness, trickery, and self-interest. Neither is concerned in the least for the welfare of animals, the planet, or the human race; both are selfishly and unashamedly antihuman to the core. As indicated in the passage I quoted above from 1 Thessalonians, both are filled with empty promises and will do much more damage than simply disappointing their deluded and dedicated followers. Both will ultimately lead them to absolute, total ruin. We will cover this in more detail later, as promised.

In 1 Timothy 6:7, we find another passage that puts the folly and foolhardy nature of these movements into perspective. It states "For we have brought nothing into the world, so we cannot take anything out of it either." It is often said in Christian circles that we can't take it with us, but we can send some on ahead, which is one basis for Christian stewardship and Christian giving. However, the search for ultimate fulfillment in this world apart from God is so strong, even today, that many will fall for that deception. This is yet another way the animal rights movement and the radical environmental movement are strongly linked. Both promise something neither is able to deliver: Satisfaction and fulfillment in this life through pursuit of something other than God. It seems noble to save the planet and its animals and ecosystems, but in their zeal to do this apart from God, and in their complete ignorance and disbelief of His Word, both movements will find nothing but devastation. As our country moves ever more in line with their philosophies, we as a nation will enter into that same kind of destruction, unless the church of Jesus Christ wakes up and begins to function as God intended to counter these movements.

Pertinent passages to this line of thinking are also found in 2 Timothy 2:23-26 and 2 Timothy 3:1-5. The first passage I have already quoted partially in the previous chapter, but more fully it states, "But refuse foolish and ignorant speculations, knowing that they produce quarrels…perhaps God may grant them repentance leading to the knowledge of the truth, and they may come to their senses and escape the snare of the devil, having been held captive by him to do his will."

Note that repentance of sin is the first prerequisite to receiving knowledge of the truth. I have yet to see on any animal rights website or in any of their publications, or those of radical environmental groups, any acknowledgement of their natural condition, that of being a sinner fully accountable to a holy God. I acknowledge my own spiritual need and the cure for my condition, and for that I receive eternal life and eternal glory. People caught up in these deceiving philosophies refuse to do so because of their own pride, the lure of the world's treasure, and Satan's trickery ("the lust of the flesh and the lust of the eyes and the boastful pride of life"—1 John 2:16). All temptation to sin falls into one of these three categories, from that of Eve in the Garden of Eden to that of Jesus Christ—and even down to us today. For this reason, both these movements beyond question receive God's condemnation and not His commendation.

The second passage from 2 Timothy states, "But realize this, that in the last days difficult times will come. For men will be lovers of self, lovers of money, boastful, arrogant, revilers, disobedient to parents, ungrateful, unholy, unloving, irreconcilable, malicious gossips, without self-control, brutal, haters of good, treacherous, reckless, conceited, lovers of pleasure rather than lovers of God; holding to a form of godliness, although they have denied its power." (3:1-5). This is in the true spirit of the antichrist, manifest in the wholesale breakdown of traditions and ignoring the keeping even of man's laws, not to mention God's. I am certain that both these movements epitomize this attitude, though doubtless, as I've stated previously, there are many sincere individuals ensnared in them because they have been deceived.

God is clear in his Word in many places, particularly in 1 John 2:15, which I also quoted earlier: "Do not love the world nor the things in the world. If anyone loves the world, the love of the Father is not in him." Nothing is to take first place over our relationship to God. If it does, it is equivalent to worshipping an idol, and God hates idolatry. The apostle John even ends his little epistle abruptly in 1 John 5:21 with the admonition, "Little children, guard yourselves from idols." Anything in our lives we place above God, manifested fully as His Son Jesus Christ is, by definition, an idol.

Doubtless those who strongly disagree with my position in these matters will ask, "Why should we even read what this guy writes?" You should read it not because it comes from me, but because it is taken directly from God's inerrant Word. If the Word is not inerrant, we have no hope of anything beyond this life. 1 John 2:25-26 states, "This is the promise which He Himself made to us: eternal life. These things I have written to you concerning those who are *trying to deceive you* [italics mine]." Let no one do this to you; use this occasion to escape the kind of deception offered in the promise of salvation through animal rights, environmental activism, a vegetarian lifestyle, or any other worldly pursuit.

I have a job serving the public, and I see so many lives that are pervaded with stark emptiness in our modern world, an emptiness that only God can fill. The corollary is that empty lives are easily filled with foolishness. That is what the animal rights movement and the radical environmental movement are all about, in their essence: Foolishness. Without the sense of a horrible, incalculable void in their lives, few people could be induced to become animal rights or environmental warriors. This is another connection between the two that is indisputable. This void is also of Satan, who is the only one who benefits from it. His counterfeit solutions are but another road to hopelessness. The only cure is the cross of Christ and the deep sense of eternal satisfaction, meaning, and purpose it provides.

So what is this spirit of antichrist to which I refer? It is deception, pure and simple, about what truly makes life meaningful and significant; it is a deception that leads people in the wrong direction. This is clearly spelled out in 2 John 1:7, which states, "For many deceivers have gone out into the world, those who do not acknowledge Jesus Christ as coming in the flesh [i.e., coming as God in the flesh—brackets mine]. This is the deceiver and the antichrist." The present participle "coming" indicates the past incarnation of Christ, His present state as a resurrected human being (and yet God), and His future return in glory to rule the world.

Jesus Himself predicted that many false christs and false prophets would come and mislead many, such as in Matthew 7:15, which states, "Beware of the false prophets who come to you in sheep's clothing, but inwardly are ravenous wolves." He repeats similar warnings in Matthew 24:11 and Mark 13:22, among other places. The specific definition of the Antichrist is found in 1 John 4:3, where it says, "Every spirit that does not confess Jesus is not from God; this is the spirit of the antichrist, of which you have heard that it is coming, and now it is already in the world." The antichrist spirit has always denied that Christ is who He claims to be: God in human flesh who paid for the sins of the world on the cross and was resurrected to show that His sacrifice was absolutely sufficient. The evolutionary and mostly godless philosophies involved in the animal rights and radical environmental movements epitomize this antichrist spirit.

The lesson for the Christian is to be on the alert for deceivers who would lead them astray. God can be trusted with the fate of the world and with the fate of the animals He created. Radical philosophies to the contrary, promoting the idea that no God will save us, that we must save ourselves, our planet, and its creatures—these are the spirit of the antichrist, and they play well into Satan's cruel and destructive hands.

NOTES

1 www.fws.gov/policy/library/(any recent year) [accessed May 2009].

2 www.aquiferguardians.org, "Another Lawsuit Filed to Stop Construction of U.S. 281 Freeway Toll Road," Feb. 26, 2008.

3 The Associated Press, "Rare Plant, Once Buried, Could Prompt Lawsuit over Highway," July 29, 2006.

4 www.tollroadsnews.com, "Enviros Bill to Stop Work on Maryland Inter-County Connector Pending Global Warming Impact Study," March 13, 2008.

5 Mark Clayton, "New Coal Plants Bury Kyoto," *The Christian Science Monitor*, Dec. 23, 2004.

6 *The New York Times*, "Fight against Coal Plants Draws Diverse Partners," Oct. 20, 2007.

7 U.S. Energy Information Administration, "Inventory of Electric Utility Power Plants in the United States."

8 Lester Brown, "USA Moving toward Ban on New Coal-Fired Plants," www.earth-policy.org, Feb. 14, 2008.

9 Jim Robbins, "Milestone Approaches in Bid to Restore the Great Plains," *The New York Times*, Nov. 17, 2005.

TWELVE

THE ROLE OF ANIMALS IN THE PREDICTED TRIBULATION

O NE of the strongest Biblical convictions I hold is that the animal rights movement is likely to play a huge destructive role during the apocalypse. They could do this by their activities releasing on humanity the unrestrained ferocity of the animal kingdom in multiple ways. Revelation 6:8 indicates that "wild beasts" will play a killing role against humanity along with famine, war, and disease, and by all these means one-fourth of the earth's population will be destroyed. Certain modern fascinations that appear to have nothing to do with animal rights may also play a role in setting the stage for this disaster. In this chapter, we will explore how this could happen.

Various Characters Who Were "Types"

All down through Bible history there have been "types" of various characters, always bearing many of the same characteristics as the one they precede, and foreshadowing the real person who is predicted to come. "Types" of Christ include the ancient king of Jerusalem in the time of Abraham, known only as Melchizedek (Genesis 14:18-20, more specifically connected to Christ in Hebrews chapters 5-7). Other types of Christ include the patriarchs Isaac and Joseph, as well as Moses. None of these is perfectly representative of the God-man they foreshadow, but they bear sufficient shared characteristics that the connection is hard to miss. There are also types of the antichrist, both in the Bible and in recent history.

An early type of the antichrist was the pharaoh of Egypt, who refused to release his Israelite slaves until God took the life of every firstborn in Egypt, including animals. Later, in 168 B.C., the Seleucid (Syrian) king Antiochus Epiphanes, whose name means "God made manifest," fulfilled many characteristics that are identical to those predicted for the Beast, as best described in Daniel 11:21-35, written hundreds of years before fulfillment by Antiochus Epiphanes. Many preterist postmillennial believers are convinced that first century Nero, the Roman Emperor prior to the destruction of Jerusalem in A.D. 70, with his vicious attacks on Christians, was the Antichrist. This is typical of a "type," which all these people were—resembling many of the characteristics of the one to come. Nevertheless, I believe that much of Daniel's prophecy following these verses concerns a ruler still yet to come who would be the dreaded final Antichrist (11:36-45), and the complete fulfillment may await the arrival of the real subject of the prophecy.

In our modern era, Adolph Hitler is the closest "type" we have to the final Antichrist, though there have been many others, and many continue to arise. Similar to Hitler are tyrants of all ages. From historic figures such as Attila the Hun, and closer to our time, petty South American dictators, Stalin, or Mao Tse-tung—the main differences between such satanically inspired bullies is their degree of ambition and level of power reached.

Hitler had many antichrist characteristics. He obviously had a "god" complex, an efficient military machine, and a desire to conquer and control the world, the same as the ultimate ruler described in Daniel 11:36-45. Hitler also reflects this prophecy in that he specialized in the capture of mighty fortresses (consider how rapidly he overran Poland and other countries and then conquered France's daunting "Maginot Line" of defense). In addition, he held a distinct hatred for the Jewish people. Many in the time of Hitler's power, in fact, thought he *was* the Antichrist; but Hitler could only be a type of that future world ruler, since he was soundly defeated in the end by the Allies.

The fact that Hitler (and many other evil people) lived a vegetarian lifestyle is vehemently denied or minimized by vegans, and there are numerous websites and books that purport to "prove" this. The facts of history are difficult to erase, however. Hitler is reliably quoted, "But there's one thing I can predict to eaters of meat: the world of the future will be vegetarian." [1]

Hitler obviously also had a problem with hunting, too, as all hunters likely were considered by him to be poachers. In that same set of papers, Hitler stated, again admitting his vegetarianism, "I am no admirer of the poacher, particularly as I am a vegetarian." [2]

He also is quoted in a different book, "Killing animals, if it must be done, is the butcher's business.... I understand, of course, that there must be professional hunters to shoot sick animals. If only there were still some danger connected with hunting, as in the days when men used spears for killing game. But today, when anybody with a fat belly can shoot the animal down at a distance.... Hunting and horse racing are the last remnants of a dead feudal world." [3] Hitler obviously never hunted mountain goats, ibex, or wild sheep, and never matched wits with a wily white-tailed deer. He probably never hunted any animal at all in his entire life.

Some of Hitler's closest associates shared this fetish for vegetarianism and animal rights, too. His propaganda minister, Joseph Goebbels, is quoted as saying, "...meat eating is a perversion in our human nature." [4] In his diary from the 1920s, Goebbels also revealed his distaste for the human race as a whole, when he stated, "As soon as I am with a person for three days, I don't like him any longer.... I have learned to despise the human being from the bottom of my soul." [4] In 1933, not long after the Nazis took over Germany, Hitler's Luftwaffe commander Herman Goering announced "an end to the 'unbearable torture and suffering in animal experiments' and threatened to 'commit to concentration camps those who still think they can continue to treat animals as inanimate property.'" [4,5] Goering called forests "God's cathedrals," echoing the mantra of John Muir, a father of the American national-park movement. [4,6] Just three years later, in 1936, a special law was passed regarding the correct way of dispatching lobsters and crabs and thus mitigating their terminal agonies. Crustaceans were to be thrown into rapidly boiling water. Bureaucrats at the Nazi Ministry of the Interior had produced learned research papers on the kindest method of killing this kind of food.[4, 7] Goebbels also reportedly stated, "The only real friend one has in the end is the dog.... The more I get to know the human species, the more I care for my Benno."[4] All these statements and acts could have easily come out of the modern animal rights movement.

Hitler had many subtle characteristics that make him seem the most accurate type of the antichrist of anyone to date. Like the predicted Antichrist, history tells us that he had little affinity for the opposite sex or for religion (consistent with Daniel 11:37). He was a vegetarian and an animal rights activist, as I believe the Antichrist may also be, especially in light of specific prophecies in the book of Revelation. Some say Hitler slaughtered multitudes of Jewish doctors on the (almost always false) charge of vivisection, or conducting surgical experiments on living animals, using these charges to mete out wholesale capital punishment. He placed severe restrictions on hunting and other uses of animals.[4] It is said that he suffered flatulence and serious digestive problems—these were most likely a result of his vegetarian lifestyle.

Convicted mass murderer Charles Manson is another vegetarian and environmental activist of which the whole vegan movement should be ashamed. His axiom was "ATWA [Air, Trees, Water, Animals, or All the Way Alive—brackets mine] is a holy war. You are either working for ATWA—life—or you're working for death." Despite his murderous bent toward human beings, Manson continued to be admired by some environmental extremists and vegans who maintained a website in his memory and, even more incredibly, in his defense.[8]

The former dictator of Cambodia, Pol Pot, head of the infamous Khmer Rouge, was another strict vegetarian with antichrist characteristics. He rose to power mainly on the strength of a poor academic record, of all things, an attribute that the anti-human Khmer Rouge considered a positive. He murdered more than two million people in the killing fields of Cambodia, many of them for the crime of simply wearing glasses, a trait that singled them out as possibly more intelligent than others.[4]

The Horrific Real Thing

Unlike these "types," the real Antichrist should fulfill all the prophecies about him (or has done so, if preterists are correct). A prominent member of the Vatican has said that he believes the Beast is living today and is "most likely now disguised as a philanthropist supporting creeds like vegetarianism, animal rights, or pacifism...."[9] I personally know of several candidates who fit this description. It appears to me that the real Antichrist could be a true fanatic when it comes to animal rights, and have a spiritual dimension from which he obtains his overarching authority. As noted below, his actual power could be granted by Satan himself, and he would promote the worship of Satan. Based on Biblical information about him, I strongly believe he could be a radical environmentalist as well, who would deceive many into thinking that in him are "peace and safety" (1 Thessalonians 5:3), while being an alarmist who betrays mankind and leads multitudes to destruction. His promises of solving all human and environmental problems and saving the planet and mankind would turn out to be empty, and his devastating seven-year reign could culminate with the return of Christ to rescue mankind from complete annihilation (Matthew 24:22).

Why do I so strongly believe these things are true? In great part, it's simply because the animal rights and environmental movements are godless in substance and evolutionary in philosophy. Both groups generally (and usually specifically) believe that man must work out his own problems because there is no personal Creator God to help us. They and their strident cries for reform could fit descriptions of the apocalypse. I also easily see that past "types" of the antichrist have espoused philosophies so very similar to those of the animal rights and environmental movements, which, if taken to the logical extreme, would have resulted in even more horror for the human race. Most of all, I believe this because their agenda seems to fit Biblical predictions, including its dreadful effect on the earth and its inhabitants.

Why would anyone subscribe to such a philosophy, with its ultimate end being inevitable hopelessness? There can only be one reason, and one place it is expressed astutely is found in 2 Corinthians 4:3-4, which states, "And even if our gospel is veiled, it is veiled to those who are perishing, in whose case the god of this world has blinded the minds of the unbelieving, that they might not see the light of the gospel of the glory of Christ, who is the image of God." Satan is many times referred to as the god or ruler of this world by Christ Himself (John 12:31; 14:30; and 16:11) as well as by others (Ephesians 2:2; 6:12; 1 John 4:4; 5:19). It seems that Satan has blinded the minds of some, causing them to oppose the very Biblical teachings that could make it plain where these sinister movements are heading. Because of this blindness, in fact, I am convinced that there will even be major opposition to what I'm stating in this book.

Let's examine what animal rights activists and, to a significant degree, some radical environmentalists espouse. They are opposed to eating animals, of course, and we have discussed the negative effects on human health that naturally arise from this perverted philosophy. Most of the world cannot survive without meat, even today, because in many countries, and even in the USA, there is a distinct lack of needed information regarding how to get the nutrients required if one doesn't consume meat. We will see shortly the verses that predict how this will play out when it is implemented worldwide by the ultimate Antichrist and his anti-human forces. If animal products were suddenly removed from the list of approved foods at the point of the Antichrist's hired guns, worldwide malnutrition would result in wholesale starvation of millions.

Concerning animal participation during the reign of the Beast, the predictions that foreshadow this begin early in the Bible, where in Leviticus 26:22, ancient Israel is warned that if they failed to keep God's Law, He would "loose among you the beasts of the field, which shall bereave you of your children and destroy your cattle and reduce your number so that your roads lie deserted." That was a very drastic reduction in population which no doubt occurred in ancient Israel as they committed exactly the sins that would bring this disaster upon them. It was also obviously a temporary reversal of the God-ordained terror He had placed on animals for man's protection after the worldwide flood (Genesis 9:2). This same terrible scenario is also predicted in Ezekiel 5:17 and in Ezekiel 14:15 and 21. God has not idly threatened how awful catastrophes involving wild beasts could reduce the human population. He has already allowed these disasters to occur, since these prophecies were about ancient Israel's downfall and have already been fulfilled.

Animal rights activists and radical environmentalists are also opposed to using animals for medical research. Any threatening new virus must be investigated by culturing it first and then attempting to develop a vaccine. Often the first antiviral medication for humans is the serum of animals rendered immune by exposure to the virus. Later comes a true vaccine most often made of neutralized virus or impotent similar virus strains. Much intensive research using live animals is necessary for effective production of any vaccine. Animal models are still absolutely necessary for this and many other medical purposes including, but not restricted to, research on cancer, heart disease, non-viral infectious diseases, testing new drugs, and even teaching medical students how to do surgery before they begin working on human beings. There is unquestionably no substitute for living tissue with circulating blood and a functioning immune system, among other things.

It is an understatement to say that the world's goods—even apart from foods and other obvious usage—consist of far more animal products than the average person realizes. Everything made from wool or silk would be excluded were all animal utilization halted. It would be a natural step to outlaw keeping of bee hives, which account for all the honey produced in the world, as well as a major percentage of pollination of plants used for food. All leather items would be eliminated. Many medicines and most cosmetics contain some form of animal product. Even cotton raised for clothing requires extensive spraying to kill attacking insects, so there would inevitably be far less (perhaps none) of that product available under the ideal animal rights ruler. Were animal rights carried to the extreme, even baking bread with yeast could be outlawed, not to mention butter and eggs. Animal products are used in myriad, subtle ways, and only when these uses are excluded would the full extent of such a loss be considered by the average person. It could become extremely difficult to obtain clothing of any kind if animal rights fanatics get their way, as I believe they may. The world could be reduced to rags in short order.

World Disarmament—A Major Key

That brings us to one final point before we go into the pertinent Scriptures. The anti-gun movement is essential in order to disarm the populace and set the stage for fulfillment of many apocalyptic prophecies. Anti-gun organizations fully comprehend that an armed individual is a citizen, while an unarmed man is a subject; and that truly free men don't have to ask for permission to bear arms. The disarmament forces have already, for the most part, effectively won the battle all over the world except in the USA. We could fall victim to it eventually, too, I believe, though organized efforts to thwart personal disarmament should continue vigorously. A disarmed population becomes helpless when faced with antagonistic wild beasts, and is powerless against the overwhelming armed forces of an oppressive government.

I travel several times a year to other countries with a hunting rifle as baggage (as I write this I happen to be on a plane from Moscow to Atlanta with a rifle in the baggage compartment), and it is treated in most places as if it were deadly poison, even though it is only a toothless collection of metal and wood until it is loaded for firing. A golf club, baseball bat, or ski pole is inherently more dangerous, in fact. Often I can't help but feel sorry for those overseas airline and border-control personnel who actually seem to be afraid of me because as an American I have the rare and precious right to travel armed. They themselves do not realize that they are already in a position of government-imposed helplessness by their lack of personal defense. There is hopeless, vulnerable disarmament all around the world even today, except for government soldiers and police, and the situation is accepted as normal in most places. In the days of the coming Antichrist this could be an absolute, irreversible fact of life for every person on planet Earth. The right to bear arms is the most direct measure of a people's freedom and, even in the USA, that freedom is under continual attack. It may be that by the time this ultimately evil leader appears and consolidates his power over the human race, only a smattering of illegitimate rebels and his trusted, omnipresent storm troopers will have firearms.

Humans as Animal Food

The first outpouring of God's fury on men who refuse to recognize Him as God comes very early in the book of Revelation, the last book of the Bible, which was penned by the apostle John early in the church age. The wrath of God against sinful, recalcitrant man begins in Revelation 6 with what is generally known as the "four horsemen of the apocalypse." In verse 8 there is an amazing and frightening statement regarding the four riders, and especially the one on the fourth horse, whose name is Death: "Authority was given to them over a fourth of the earth, to kill with sword and with famine and with pestilence and by *the wild beasts of the earth* [italics mine]." At the very start of what is known in eschatology as the Tribulation Period, it says that these four disasters will kill one-fourth of the population of the world. Many people dismiss the last of these, if not the whole section, but I believe wild beasts could be prevalent enough to kill many millions of people in that terrible time.

For one thing, the special relationship of the animal rights movement to predators is well known. As previously covered, we are seeing wolves reestablished in places where they were formerly subdued and removed decades or even centuries ago, and any attempt to control their numbers today is vigorously opposed by animal rights groups. There are now many wolves in the Lower Forty-eight of the USA, and they are being reintroduced into the southern Rocky Mountains and Mexico. It is only a matter of time before packs start appearing along the East Coast. The Alps of Europe now have wolves in places they haven't been found for centuries. I recently killed wolves in both Romania and Mongolia, which have robust populations of these predators that are a huge problem as they threaten livestock, other wildlife, and people.

The brown bear of Eurasia continues to expand its range into areas from which it was extirpated long ago. The black bear of the Americas now raids garbage cans at suburban, and even urban, homes in almost every state in the union. Mountain lions have been hunted in sustainable fashion in North America for many years, but numerous states have caved to animal rights propaganda and established major obstacles or prohibitions against any logical control of their numbers. Naturally, people are now losing children and pets to them, and fatal attacks on adults occur fairly regularly. Mountain lions (cougars) are now appearing in eastern North America, too, either naturally expanding their range or being brought in from other places and released illegally by unknown persons. Alligators have made a comeback that has put them on golf courses and in backyard ponds from Florida to Texas to North Carolina. Animal rights groups and radical environmentalists play the same tune, such as "you're more likely to be struck by lightening than be killed by a mountain lion." What they don't realize is that these increasingly common attacks foreshadow a possible removal of the God-imposed "terror" of mankind that dates all the way back to Genesis 9:2.

Under normal circumstances, a good case could be made that some of these restockings are good conservation moves, and there is an element of truth to it. However, restocking or expanding ranges of predators must be accompanied by appropriate management measures (which means issuing permits to kill as many of them as necessary, for those who miss my point). The time of the Tribulation predicted in the Bible would not be a normal circumstance, however. It would be a time when, I believe, the post-flood terror necessary for human survival, placed supernaturally by God on all these creatures, would be removed. While I can't say exactly when this might occur, there is indication that it could happen at some point after God removes His people (the church, another way of saying all those who believe in Christ for salvation, whatever their organizational affiliation) in what is generally referred to as the Rapture (1 Thessalonians 4:16-17). It is also quite possible that this removal could occur later in the Tribulation, or even afterward, and that God may choose to allow some of His own people to be victims of these animal attacks.

A recent newspaper article out of Iraq is unintentionally supportive of this interpretation of Revelation. It confirms that "something strange happened this year. Locals believe the wolves must have crossed some threshold of desperation or hunger, reached a tipping point that had previously prevented them from venturing onto human turf. They overcame their fear of people and began entering towns and villages to feast on sheep and cattle. Animal experts say predatory beasts such as wolves overcome their fear of humans when they're in close proximity to them. Some farmers speculated that the wolves had migrated from deserts to the villages because of three years of sparse rains and a lack of suitable prey. Others, including the local vet, said the incursions began after nomadic tribes began using high fences to protect their livestock. 'The wolves are fierce because of hunger and thirst that plagued them,' said Abu Kaheela [a veterinarian—brackets mine]. 'That is why they began showing no fear.'" [10]

Despite how disturbing this scenario, it could be but a specter of more terrible times to come. Few would dispute that we are seeing a radical upswing in the numbers of attacks by wild animals on human beings. Even circus and performing animals seem to be "going crazy" far more frequently than in times past. Black bear and grizzly bear attacks are up almost everywhere these animals roam, and mountain lion assaults on people are especially frequent. In 2007, there were seven documented attacks by grizzly bears on hunters in Montana alone.[11] Shark attacks along many coasts are at record highs. Environmentalists, as one would expect, blame the human population for invading territory traditionally occupied by these animals, but man has historically appropriated and occupied such areas with little danger of being victimized by animals. To me, these recent onslaughts by animals have a definite apocalyptic feel to them, as wild creatures unwittingly foreshadow the major role they may play for Satan's Antichrist during the Tribulation.

People may not feel at all safe from animal attacks during such an awful period, even if they live in an urban area without any significant population of predators nearby. The Beast of Revelation might consider it an abomination for people to "own" animals as pets, and those with pets wouldn't be able to make that relationship acceptable by referring to themselves as "guardians." Likely they would be required to release their dogs, cats, canaries, and iguanas from their "prisons," and these animals would suddenly be forced to fend for themselves. Dogs would particularly be a factor as they form vicious packs, weed out weaker animals by devouring them, and then begin preying on people. Zoo animals such as lions and tigers, as well as lesser cats and bears, could be released on inviolable orders from the world leader. These creatures would have absolutely no fear of people, and could likely kill thousands of human beings in large cities worldwide the very first day of their "freedom."

UFOs and the Tribulation

If the removal of Christians occurs in the manner that proponents of the Rapture expect (as mentioned earlier in this text), it may be a prominent event that surprises and astonishes many. However, it could be that the number of followers of Christ will be relatively small and their absence hardly noticed at all. If it does send shock waves throughout the world, the event would likely be blamed on some kind of alien lifeform removing large numbers of human beings.

I believe the near-manic search for extraterrestrial life may be somehow related to this. All indications are that the billions of dollars spent on that futile effort have been a total waste of time and resources akin to the plethora of mostly useless environmental laws taxpayers have funded for decades. Unidentified flying objects (UFOs) may exist, but it appears more likely that these are deceiving angels (demons), perhaps preparing an explanation for occurrence of the Rapture, a coming event about which they may be already fully aware. After all, Satan is also called "the prince of the power of the air" (Ephesians 2:2), so such sightings would be in keeping with his dominion and his nature. They are unlikely to be alien creatures from some advanced planet remote from this world; what if instead, they already live here? If what I believe is true, there is indeed extraterrestrial life in the form of God and His angels. Satan was "cast down" and may be confined to this world, which some believe was originally prepared as a habitation for him and his fallen angels (Revelation 12:9).

So what does this have to do with animal rights? If extraterrestrial life can be found, it would be far more than a monumental scientific achievement. It would provide a naturalistic explanation for all creation, as well as presumptive proof that life can arise apart from God's creative hand—at least that's how evolutionists would see it. The animal rights movement in its essence is predicated on the equality of human beings and animals because they share a common ancestor. It is on this basis alone that their "equality" premise stands or falls.

It is certainly clear that if God's Word is believed, it leaves no room whatsoever for the concept of animal rights, nor, in my opinion, extraterrestrial life. Such sci-fi material is completely out of the question because it is predicated on evolution, which I have already shown is a demonstrably bogus concept altogether. While I enjoyed *E. T., Star Wars,* and *Independence Day* as entertainment, should intelligent extraterrestrial life ever prove to be fact, the animal rights movement would have a much stronger case!

Back to the Beast Feast

In any event, many things point to the possibility that during the Tribulation, for the first time since the flood of Noah, animals would have no fear at all of human beings. A mountain lion could routinely stalk and kill a person as if they were a deer or an elk. Black and grizzly bears might break into houses not for canned food or other pantry items, but for human flesh. Polar bears, which even now exist in record numbers, could decimate and possibly wipe out the human population of the Arctic. Packs of sharp-fanged wild dogs in the cities could kill at will. Millions of human beings could fall victim to rampaging predators, and they would have neither the arms nor the knowledge to counter them. It would be human slaughter, and the carnage might be appreciated, applauded, and encouraged by the ultimate animal rights activist and environmentalist, the Beast. He would be delighted as the human population plunges toward half-billion, the ideal touted by some population control activists.

No Animal Products Equals Famine

Another huge killing circumstance during the Tribulation would be famine (Revelation 6:6, 8). Like the Nazis, except to an infinitely stricter degree, the Antichrist could move the population toward radical vegetarianism. I believe he might mandate it very early in his reign and enforce it with arms, and nobody would have the power to oppose his decree. It is asked in Revelation 13:4, "Who is like the Beast, and who is able to wage war with him?" Nobody would be anything like him among other human beings and, by the time he seizes absolute power, nobody would have sufficient means to make war with him. He could be empowered by Satan himself, according to that same Scripture passage.

One need only imagine what would happen when meat, even that of lowly insects, is suddenly excluded from the human diet by irrevocable mandate from the Antichrist. Malnutrition could kill millions, particularly in parts of the world where nutritional information is not readily available. Unless there is a supply of data regarding how to obtain the missing ingredients such as vitamin B12, iron, and certain amino acids, this time would herald a worldwide famine of unparalleled proportions. Under the Antichrist, with his strong environmentalist and animal rights credentials, with his well-armed storm troopers to enforce his decrees, and considering he may have an overwhelming yearning to reduce the human population dramatically, such public-service information won't be provided anywhere in the world. Famine may likely be made more severe by rigorous restrictions on large-scale farming methods that are designed to protect insects from harm.

Other Killing Factors

Disease follows famine wherever it occurs, but in a brave new world ruled by Satan's animal rights/environmentalist savior, both old and new diseases could crop up with extreme regularity, again killing millions. Since animal research would be among the first practices banned (as it was under Hitler in Germany), there would be no hope of help. In the absence of medications and good advice, even minor diseases could wash like a tide through the population, and death would be so common that people could become completely calloused by it.

The final component might be war (Revelation 6:4), which could occur for several reasons. Some means of resisting the oppressive world authority may still exist, but those who attempt this would be dealt with ruthlessly. Success against the world government by poorly-armed and poorly-equipped rebels would be highly elusive and practically impossible. There could likely be some recalcitrant nations, as well, with which the all-powerful Antichrist must deal forcefully. Many Bible scholars are convinced that the nation Israel would be the final holdout (Zechariah 12:8-10, for example). According to this dispensational interpretation, they could be nearly surrounded and close to annihilation during the Tribulation period, but, in the end, their Messiah, Jesus Christ, would return at their hour of greatest need to save them. Only then would all Jews who remain alive recognize the monstrous deception they have long believed and, with grief-stricken hearts, welcome Him as Lord and King (verse 12:10).

The traditional dispensational interpretation is that the Jews will rebuild their temple in Jerusalem as the time of Satan's dominion approaches. Many believe that when the Antichrist strikes a deal with Israel to allow reinstitution of temple worship, the actual Tribulation begins (Daniel 9:25-27). In prophetic terms, the week referred to in this passage would have to mean a "week of years," or seven years. According to this interpretation, during the initial three-and-a-half years after his treaty with Israel, the Antichrist would likely be putting down rebellion elsewhere and consolidating his power, while in effect honoring his covenant with Israel. A plausible scenario would be that "in the middle of the week," after this initial three-and-a-half-year period has passed, the Beast will become enraged at ongoing animal sacrifices in the temple and, by force, will put a stop to the practice, setting himself up in the temple to be worshipped in place of God (this would constitute the "abomination of desolation" spoken of by Christ in Matthew 24:15, the first one documented since that of Antiochus Epiphanes in 168 B.C.). Exactly how all this could play out is not specifically revealed in the Bible but, if the premillennial view is correct, it seems likely that eventually the Antichrist will focus all his forces on Israel when they resist by their own force of arms (Revelation 16:14-16). The major factor initiating the final Battle of Armageddon, in fact, could well be the Antichrist's strong sentiment for animal rights!

Two other animals to which I must allude are mentioned in Revelation. One is the "flying scorpions" of Revelation 9:3-10, which says they will inflict horrible suffering on the human race for five months. Their description is very specific and it is frightening. These creatures could be demonic in nature but have many characteristics of insects. In this unusual physical form they apparently have a limited lifespan, much like insects, but while they are present, cause much agony.

The final animal I want to cover is the lowly vulture. While most of the wildlife of the earth may perish during the awful events of the Tribulation, the vulture might prosper. Its main food could be human beings, whose bodies would be available by the hundreds of millions, and perhaps by the billions. That these birds would then have a feast is quite specifically predicted in the Old Testament in Ezekiel 39:17-20, and in the New Testament in Revelation 19:17-18 and 19:21. The carnage that characterizes the whole book of Revelation could surely lead to a tremendous proliferation of carrion-eating birds. It is interesting and intriguing that the wrath of God on the earth seems to be marked as finished only when the vultures have eaten their fill of human flesh. It isn't a pretty scenario until one reaches the last two chapters, Revelation 20 and 21, wherein Jesus Christ establishes His earthly Kingdom and all the Biblical promises to believers begin to unfold.

It doubtless sounds paradoxical to many but, in the Biblical record, animal rights and radical environmentalism have no important function except as destroyers. They do have their role to play, but it appears decidedly apocalyptic. God help those who adhere to these distorted philosophies and refuse to change their minds.

NOTES

1 *Hitler's Table Talk: Secret Conversations*, edited by H. R. Trevor-Roper, Nov. 11, 1941, Section 66, 122-124.

2 *Hitler's Table Talk: Secret Conversations*, edited by H. R. Trevor-Roper, Aug. 20, 1942, Section 293.

3 Albert Speer, *Inside the Third Reich*, Simon & Schuster Inc., 1970, Chapter 7.

4 www.vegetariansareevil.com/hitler, [accessed February 2009].

5 Alexander Cockburn, "Vegetarians, Nazis for Animal Rights, Blitzkrieg of the Ungulates," Aug. 18, 2005, www.counterpunch.org/cockburn08182005.html, [accessed February 2009].

6 Kaltio, February 2003, *Animal Rights in the Third Reich (Aslak Aikio)*, www.kaltio.fi/index.php?494, [accessed February 2009].

7 Dennis Prager, "Kindness to Animals = Cruelty Towards Humans?" July 24, 2007, www.worldnetdaily.com/index.php?pageId=42710 [accessed May 2009].

8 www.atwa.info, [not currently working]; www.mansondirect.com/updates.html "The official site for Charles Manson truth," [accessed February 2009].

9 Cardinal Giacomo Biffi, BBC News Europe, March 6, 2000, "Cardinal: Antichrist Is a Vegetarian."

10 Abu Kaheela, March 17, 2008, *The Los Angeles Times*, "Hungry Wolves Attack Livestock in Iraq."

11 Keith McCafferty, "The Grizzly Storm," *Field & Stream*, Feb. 2008, 15-16.

THIRTEEN

FINAL THOUGHTS

MANY will no doubt question and condemn severely what I have written in this book. I expect these critics to attempt to explain away the obvious indictment of the animal rights/vegetarian/radical environmentalist movements by the Holy Scriptures. In response I offer the passage recorded in Matthew 22:29, the words of Jesus Christ, where He stated to His opponents, "You are mistaken, not understanding the Scriptures or the power of God." This statement was made to the Sadducees, Jewish leaders who maintained that there was nothing supernatural in the world and that there is no resurrection of the dead. They were the humanists and skeptics of their day. What Jesus said to them remains as true today as when it was spoken, and it applies directly to modern-day philosophies that mimic such erroneous beliefs.

It was another of Hitler's henchmen, Joseph Goebbels, who best described today's animal rights movement. He stated, referring primarily to all Nazi propaganda, "If you tell a lie big enough, people will eventually come to believe it…the truth is the mortal enemy of the lie…and thus by extension the truth is the greatest enemy of the state."[1]

Today's animal rights movement holds the same kind of worldly viewpoint, and has its origins in godless evolution and humanism. Some in that movement recognize clearly the dichotomy between their position and the diametrically opposing God-centered philosophy.

Dr. Peter Singer, a noted author and the father of the modern animal rights movement, who holds the high-sounding title of DeCamp Professor of Bioethics at Princeton University, states, "Christianity is our foe. If animal rights is to succeed, we must destroy the Judeo-Christian religious tradition."[2]

The important point that must be emphasized is this: The animal rights movement has nothing at all to do with being kind to animals. It is anti-human in its essence, violent at its core, and capable of anything to advance its agenda and thwart its adversaries. Its only real program is to grow by increasing contributions, political influence, and power. While I hope no physical harm comes at their hands to any of their opponents, I personally refuse to be afraid of them or anything else in this world because, as God's word instructs, "God has not given us a spirit of timidity [fear], but of power and love and of self-discipline" (2 Timothy 1:7, brackets mine). It is too late for anyone to prevent me from having what Christ promised to all who follow Him—the abundant life. I believe my life has already been well spent for the most part, and I confidently place myself in God's loving care for whatever He has in store for me. I have often said that there is nothing I fear except depending on myself and insisting on my own agenda; it is infinitely better to depend on God and His agenda. He is able to protect, and He is able to destroy or allow destruction. In any event, I hope to leave this life in the center of His will, however that event occurs.

I hope it is not too much to expect that at least some people will read this work and come to their senses and escape deception. However, I already know that self-willed, rebellious people will assuredly remain that way, unless the Holy Spirit of God intervenes and opens their eyes. Blindness is a terrible state of affairs, but to be willfully blind is even worse. The cure really is a supernatural act over which man has no control. Only those regenerated by believing in Jesus Christ, people in whom the Holy Spirit dwells, are truly capable of understanding and digesting what I have written. As noted earlier, it says in 1 Corinthians 2:14-16, "A natural man does not accept the things of the Spirit of God; for they are foolishness to him, and he cannot understand them, because they are spiritually appraised." Even some Christians may take issue with me on some points, because there is doubtless latitude for disagreement here and there. Nevertheless, I believe that what I have written is defensible and reasonable, because it is solidly based on the integrity of the Word of God.

I would be remiss if I didn't take this opportunity to present the real truth about how to live a complete life, regardless of your current philosophy, health, economic status, ethnicity, sex, age, or any other factor. It certainly is not through fervently believing in and following some worldly cause such as animal rights or saving the environment. Individuals must first recognize themselves for what they are: sinners. Romans 3:23 tells us, "for all have sinned and fall short of the glory of God." However, God in His great mercy wasn't willing to leave us without hope, for in Romans 6:23 He states in His Word, "For the wages of sin is death, but the free gift of God is eternal life in Jesus Christ our Lord." Romans 5:8 reveals how great God's mercy is when it says, "But God demonstrates His own love toward us, in that while we were yet sinners, Christ died for us." Romans 10:9 tells us how to appropriate God's love in Christ when it gives the formula, "if you confess with your mouth Jesus as Lord, and believe in your heart that God raised Him from the dead, you shall be saved." Once you do this you can face the future with confidence, since the little book of 1 John tells us in 5:11-12, "And the testimony is this, that God has given us eternal life, and this life is in His Son. He who has the Son has the life; he who does not have the Son of God does not have the life."

Postmillennial eschatology expects the church, under leadership of God Himself in the person of the Holy Spirit, to triumph over all these foes and usher in all the promises to believers found in the Bible. They believe that most (or all) apocalyptic prophecies were fulfilled with the Roman destruction of Jerusalem in A.D. 70. I hope this interpretation is right, and that many of the awful predictions have already come to pass. I also hope the church will awaken and win the world to Jesus Christ, and that the church victorious will see all Christ's enemies made into His footstool (Psalm 110:1). The ideal would be Christ triumphant and mankind totally converted by the Holy Spirit using the victorious church as His effective vehicle of change. If we fail in this as Christians, it is not a failure of the Holy Spirit, any more than failure of the Mosaic Law and the Jewish nation to diligently and fully reveal God to the world can be construed as a failure of God Himself. To me, such would be only an-other sign of man's absolute helplessness and total depravity, even though all true believers house within our persons the indwelling Holy Spirit.

However and whenever Christ's Kingdom is fully ushered in, there is hope for all mankind. Even for extremist animal rights activists and environmental warriors, I would offer them this eternal hope that they surely won't find in their current worldview, no matter how hard they try and no matter how successful they appear to be. The tainted creation they now worship will indeed be redeemed and purified someday. They, too, can know the God and Christ that I serve, and be assured that renewal and restoration of the earth will come to pass without extreme measures on their part to save animals and the environment. In Romans 8:18-23, the Bible speaks of how the creation itself groans and suffers under the weight of man's sin while awaiting redemption. Above all, it is so important that people not exchange the truth of God for a lie, and not worship and serve the creature rather than the Creator, who is blessed forever (Romans 1:25). To do so is nothing less than blindness and sin—as well as idolatry.

If you have never done so, I urge you to take the appropriate steps today. If you willfully choose to remain an atheist or simply a skeptic and determine in your heart that you are right and I am wrong, I have lost nothing. However, if I am right and you are wrong, you have lost everything. That simple formula should at least be cause for the intel-ligent person to investigate further the claims of Jesus Christ.

As for me, I submit this work only in the hopes that it will be useful in promoting understanding of the real issues at stake. I hope someone, somewhere, will learn the truth from reading it. It is self-evident that not everyone will agree with me, but even if I should become extremely unpopular because of this book, I have comfort directly from God's Word. Jesus Christ said in John 15:19, "If you were of the world, the world would love its own; but because you are not of the world…the world hates you." The apostle John repeats this same theme in 1 John 3:13: "Do not be surprised…if the world hates you." Christians should seriously take stock of how they are living if they obtain tremendous accolades from the world at large.

Even if the world hates me, I count myself blessed to be able to visualize and record the things in this book. May God satisfy you with truth and grace if you are blessed by them, too.

Notes

1   www.thinkexist.com/quotation/joseph_goebbels [accessed Feb. 2009].

2   www.caare101.org/anti_human_quotes.htm [accessed February 2009], *The DeWeese Report,* Nov. 1998.

APPENDIX

WILD GAME RECIPES FROM THE KITCHEN OF A HUNTER'S WIFE

by Linda Jones

Prologue

IT was probably inevitable that I would learn to cook wild game, since I've been married to a dedicated hunter for 45 years. It has actually been a joyful journey as we have eaten wild game from all over North America through the years. While J. Y. was in medical school and I was working as a low-salary junior high school teacher, we were exceedingly poor, and no economic help was possible from either of our families. I learned to cook frog legs, quail, doves, and various varieties of fish, so our young family stayed well-nourished. Years later, when J. Y. started hunting big game, I learned to cook deer (now our staple), pronghorn antelope, elk, moose, wild sheep, and many other animals. J. Y. did his part by learning how to best prepare these animals after the kill so they would be prime meat for my kitchen. When I select a cut of wild meat from my freezer for cooking, I know that it has been killed cleanly with a well-placed shot that destroys little edible meat. It has been promptly field-dressed, with the intestines and blood removed right away to cool the meat and prevent any offensive taste from clinging to it. Unfortunately, too many hunters in this modern era are ignorant of what to do after the kill to assure the very best in wild game for the kitchen, and my advice from experience is that they do whatever is necessary to learn these essential outdoor skills.

After the animal has been promptly skinned, something J. Y. does in minutes, it is hung in our walk-in cooler where it stays at 39° Fahrenheit for up to ten days while it "ages" and becomes even tenderer. J. Y. then processes it himself in our meat processing facility, which is adjacent to our cooler and has all the necessary implements to do a good job. He cuts the meat into three basic types: ground deer, cubed deer, and a variety of roast cuts. The ground deer is pure red meat with no additives, and even when grilled as hamburgers it stays together remarkably well. It is invaluable as a substitute for ground beef for any application that calls for this commodity. The best feature of such meat is that I know exactly how it was cared for and prepared, and that it contains no antibiotics, hormones, or other unknown chemicals, which is much more than I know about any meat from my local grocery store.

Below are a few of my favorite recipes, but keep in mind that most wild meat can be substituted in your own recipes that call for market meat such as beef, pork, etc. If your meat is as well prepared as mine, you really don't need any special recipes.

VEGETABLE STIR-FRY

1–2 pounds of venison, cut into 1-inch cubes
¼ to ½ cup soy sauce
2 cloves garlic, crushed

Combine these in a plastic zip-lock bag and marinate in the refrigerator for two or three hours. In the meantime, prepare your favorite vegetables to stir-fry. I usually use a color palette of green, red, yellow, and white vegetables. You may use as many or as few as you like. I always include onion for the flavor it imparts to the stir-fry. Cut each vegetable into bite-size pieces. When you are ready to cook, pour ¼ cup of olive oil in a wok or large skillet and heat the oil on medium high until it is hot. Remove your marinated meat from the fridge and drain away and discard the marinade. Cook the meat for two or three minutes or until brown. Remove it from the wok or skillet and place it somewhere to keep it warm. Stir in the vegetables and cook only until they are tender but still crisp. Return the meat to the cooking utensil and heat it together with the vegetables until all is hot. Serve over cooked brown rice with extra soy sauce. This serves about four people.

DEER ROAST

1 small deer roast, two pounds or less
Salt and pepper or your favorite seasoning
⅛ cup olive oil, for searing

Wash and dry the roast. Season it all over with salt and pepper (or your favorite seasoning) and rub it into the meat well. Heat the olive oil in a cast-iron skillet (this is best, but whatever you have will suffice) until it is hot. Sear the roast on all sides until it is brown. Pre-heat your oven to 350°, and place it in the oven (leave it in the skillet) for about twenty minutes. Check the temperature several times with an instant-read thermometer. The roast is done when the thermometer registers 150°–160°, at which point it will be medium rare to medium. Do not overcook, as deer is very lean and can be tough if it is cooked too long. Let the roast stand for 15 minutes before you slice and serve. A small roast such as this will shrink some, so it serves two people.

ANABEL'S MARINADE FOR WILD GAME

2½ cups dry red wine

1 cup olive oil

2 lemons, juiced

2 celery stalks, coarsely chopped

3 stalks fresh parsley

2 sprigs fresh thyme

2 bay leaves

1–2 tablespoons black peppercorns, crushed

MIX all these ingredients together and store in the refrigerator. It is good for up to two weeks. This marinade is excellent for large game like elk or moose. An excellent choice is an elk tenderloin, which should be marinated overnight. It should then be prepared exactly as the deer roast was prepared in the previous recipe, adjusting roasting time according to the size of the cut. Do not cook to a temperature over 160° Fahrenheit.

A Few More Pointers

Don't be afraid to experiment with flavors and recipes. Wild meat of any kind is far more flavorful than its average farm-raised counterpart. Also, as previously mentioned, it has no unknown additives such as hormones or other medicines, since it is completely wild and free-ranging. I consider it far more healthful than farm-raised meat. Try ground deer in your favorite chili, spaghetti, or hamburger recipes.

Wild boar—and most wild meats—make wonderful sausage, if your inclinations are in that direction. The tender loins of pork (the center of the pork chop, which J. Y. removes in a long, single delicious piece) can be cooked by whatever recipe you have on hand, as you can hardly miss with this one. If you are fortunate enough to obtain a wild turkey, roast it longer and slower than you would the domestic variety. It takes a lot of oil, but another way to get the best from a wild turkey is to deep-fry it (such as in a large fish cooker).

Be creative and unafraid and you will assuredly find out just how excellent these meats really are.

SCRIPTURE
INDEX

ABOUT THE AUTHOR

PHOTO BY LINDA JONES

J. Y.
JONES
M.D.

THIS is the sixth non-fiction book by Dr. J. Y. Jones, an avid writer who has also written more than two hundred fifty articles for magazines and other periodicals. Jones is a committed evangelical Christian who takes seriously the call to live a holy life that honors the Lord Jesus Christ. Most of his writing has been for outdoors enthusiasts, although he has also written two fiction novels with a third nearing completion. His avocation is hunting, and he has been involved in outdoor pursuits since childhood. He has taken all species and subspecies of North American big game using the same Remington .30-06 rifle, and is in the process of repeating this accomplishment in Europe and Asia, where he hopes to take all available species with another Remington rifle. His North American book, *One Man, One Rifle, One Land* (Safari Press, 2001), is considered by many to be the definitive work on North American big-game hunting and is in its second printing. Jones's book on Eurasia will be titled *Another Rifle, Another Land*, and should also be another highly authoritative tome on hunting that part of the world. His credentials in North American hunting have opened many doors as he approached dozens of guides to participate in Safari Press's *Ask the Guides* series of books, the most successful series of North American hunting books that publishing house has ever printed. *Ask the Brown Bear/Grizzly Guides* is in press and will be his tenth book. Jones is also a regular contributor to *Sports Afield* magazine, among other publications. An eye physician and surgeon (ophthalmologist) who has practiced for four decades, Jones is a decorated Vietnam veteran and a member of many hunting and conservation organizations. He has received numerous awards for writing and photography. Jones initiated the Sportsmen's Prayer Breakfast, which has spread far beyond the initial event at the Safari Club International Convention in 1995, where he was its first speaker. He is a frequent speaker at wild-game suppers and other sportsmen's events, and particularly enjoys sharing his Christian testimony. He has participated in twenty-three overseas eye-surgery mission trips, primarily to Honduras and Jamaica. He is fluent in Spanish and conversational in Russian. He has been married to his wife, Linda, since 1964.

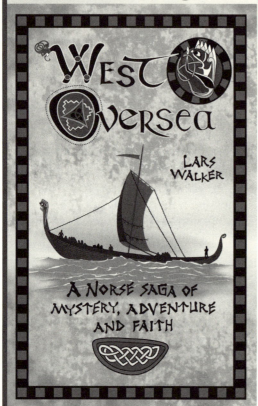

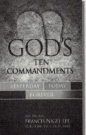

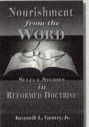
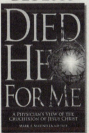

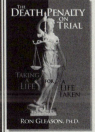
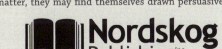